MEDITERRANEAN DIET

BEST RECIPES FOR

HEALTHY WEIGHT LOSS

YOUR HEALTHY EATING COOKBOOK

DELICIOUS AND EASY HEALTHY RECIPES

Copyright, Legal Notice and Disclaimer:

This publication is protected under the US Copyright Act of 1976 and all other applicable international, federal, state and local laws, and all rights are reserved, including resale rights: you are not allowed to give or sell this Guide to anyone else.

Please note that much of this publication is based on research, personal experience and anecdotal evidence. Although the author and publisher have made every reasonable attempt to achieve complete accuracy of the content in this Guide, they assume no responsibility for errors or omissions. Also, you should use this information as you see fit, and at your own risk. Your particular situation may not be exactly suited to the examples illustrated here; in fact, it's likely that they won't be the same, and you should adjust your use of the information and recommendations accordingly.

Any trademarks, service marks, product names or named features are assumed to be the property of their respective owners, and are used only for reference. There is no implied endorsement if we use one of these terms.

Finally, use your head. Nothing in this Guide is intended to replace common sense, legal, medical or other professional advice, and is meant to inform and entertain the reader. So have fun with this MEDITERRANEAN DIET COOKBOOK.

Copyright © 2014 Mario Fortunato. All rights reserved worldwide.

Table of Content

- History and Tradition of the Mediterranean Diet
- Discover the Benefits of the Mediterranean Diet for Your Health and Healthy Weight Loss
- Healthy and Powerful Tips to Easily Adopt a Mediterranean Lifestyle Now
- Collection of the Best Mediterranean Diet Recipes
- Get Inspired With a Mediterranean Diet Breakfast
- Healthy Mediterranean Diet Salad Recipes
- More Delicious and Healthy Recipes & Tips
- How Much Weight Can You Lose With a Mediterranean Diet

- Discover the Health and Fitness Benefits of Red Wine
- Discover the Health Powers of Olive Oil

HISTORY AND TRADITION OF THE MEDITERRANEAN DIET

The Mediterranean diet, as it is known, is a diet whose history and tradition is rich with the throes of European history, and specifically southern European cuisine, culture, and more. Starting in Italy, and spreading to Greece, Spain, and other areas around the Mediterranean, including those around the sea itself, this diet has been successful all over the world. Not only as a tasty way to eat, drink, and live but also as a realistic way to lose and manage weight in a professional and sustainable way.

The diet follows the historic and traditional eating and social patterns of the regions around southern Italy, Greece, and Spain while providing for people the option to eat, drink and be merry – literally – with a wide array of foods and wines to choose from in a tasty manner!

THE MEDITERRANEAN REGION
& THE DELICIOUS MEDITERRANEAN DIET

The diet primarily and uniquely consists of foods and ingredients such as olive oil, legumes such as peas and beans, fruits, vegetables, and unrefined cereal products as seen in some of the recipes included in this book. Another major staple of the diet is fish, and a moderate consumption of cheeses and yogurts are included as a way to receive healthy fats and cholesterol.

Fish products are a central part of the diet itself, as it stays away from the more traditional meat products, promoting only a small consumption on meats and heavier meals – instead going for the lighter and healthier fish options across the board. This, in part, leads to healthier lifestyles for those looking to lose weight and improve things such as their cholesterol, their heart health, and their weight management abilities.

In addition, the history of the Mediterranean diet includes a love for and fascination with wine – with wine and fine alcohols making themselves a staple of the diet and an important part of getting the most out of the diet and meals themselves over time.

The diet took hold around the world in the 1990s, when a Harvard University doctor showcased it as a diet that had the potential to help people to lose weight and improve adherence to nutritional guidelines in time. Since then, people struggling with weight loss have turned to the Mediterranean diet with great success and enjoyable results.

The diet focuses on a consumption of healthy fats while keeping carbohydrates relatively low and improving a person's intake of protein, while also giving a person the option to lose weight in a healthy way with a high amount of seafood. That seafood, containing healthy fatty acids that the body needs, works to help manage weight and improve energy levels, among other things.

In all, the diet is a perfect option for people seeking to improve their health while getting the most out of their outlook regarding a sustainable lifestyle choice that they can make and stick with regarding weight loss. The diet is both sustainable and worthwhile, and has been undertaken by many people all around the world with great success related to weight loss and more, as it works to help manage weight and reduce fat intake naturally and easily.

Discover the Benefits of the Mediterranean Diet for Your Health and Healthy Weight Loss

It is not just popular because most celebrities are practicing it or because it has an associated class and a note of luxury and abundance. The Mediterranean diet is widespread and highly effective because it introduces a way of life healthy and holds the key to longevity and satisfaction when maintained. Another influencing factor is that it can encourage people to come together and bond over a very healthy meal.

Components of the Mediterranean Diet

The Mediterranean diet has long been one of the healthiest diets known to man because for thousands of years citizens along the Mediterranean coast have indulged in fruits, vegetables, grains, and a glass of wine to complete a meal. It is not just a diet but a way of life. Those who have practiced the diet also have the luxury of leisurely dining, delicious foods, and engaging in regular physical activity. This smart choice of a healthy way of life leads to longer lives free of chronic complications and diseases.

Based on research, one such diet rich in plant-based foods and healthy fat is good for you. It also further supports that this particular diet can protect against the development of heart disease, metabolic complications, cancer, Type 2 Diabetes, obesity, dementia, Alzheimer's, and Parkinson's.

The positive results of this particular diet have been studied for over ten years providing better evidence. It also has a link to protect from diabetes and cardiovascular disease. It is the whole package, not just the diet alone that contributes to overall wellness. The diet greatly comprises of delicious foods nutrient rich, and the physical activity as well as the sharing of meals with loved ones is an added plus.

I am Overweight...

If you are overweight, you can start the Mediterranean diet and begin enjoying its benefits as there are adverse health effects with staying obese. These include hypertension, knee arthritis, strokes, heart attacks, Type 2

Diabetes, cancer and premature death. Losing weight can help to prevent some of these complications.

In itself, the Mediterranean diet is not a weight loss program. It is the habitual careful selection of what you are putting inside your body that is linked with longer life spans and lower rates of chronic illnesses that could otherwise mean costlier treatments. The list of possible complications includes cardiovascular disease, cancers, and dementia. The diet is also linked to asthma control and prevented cases of diabetes and Parkinson's. There is no other diet that can claim these benefits.

The mantra when losing weight effectively would have to be to lose excess weight and consume food carefully and wisely. If you are intent on losing weight, you can do it this way, and you can start sooner than you think. The **best Mediterranean recipes** have been compiled in this book to help you with your weight loss program and to help you start living a healthy eating lifestyle.

If you do not take care in what you eat and do not lose weight, the list of complications includes:

- Obstructive sleep apnea
- Gallstones
- Hypertension

- Higher cholesterol count, which could lead to hardening of the arteries
- Increased cancers
- Strokes
- Pain in the lower back
- Varicose veins
- Hemorrhoids
- Blood clots in legs and lungs
- Poor wound healing
- Surgery complications
- Wound infection
- Breathing problems
- Pregnancy complications
- Fat build up in the liver
- Asthma
- Low sperm count
- Decreased fertility
- Delayed or missed diagnosis

Isn't this list quite intimidating to look at?

Weight Loss Secrets

This type of diet aims to regulate weight loss, keep your heart and brain in check, prevent cancer, and prevent diabetes if not control it. You can lose weight, keep it off, and avoid chronic diseases. The best thing about this type of diet, which is surprisingly the same with other cultures, is that it emphasizes the consumption of fresh fruits and vegetables, whole grains, nuts, beans, olive oil, herbs and spices, and eating fish and seafood at least twice a week. Poultry, eggs, cheese, and yogurt also can be consumed in moderation, whereas sweets and red meat are consumed for special occasions. A daily glass of red wine is highly encouraged along with daily physical activity.

THE MEDITERRANEAN DIET PYRAMID

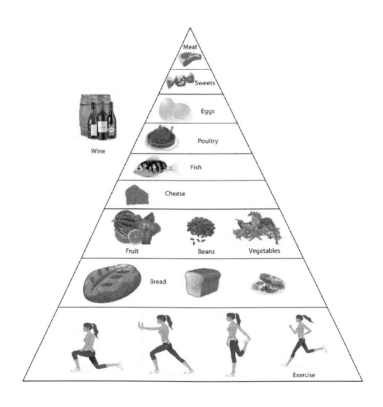

MEDITERRANEAN DIET

Mediterranean Foods Category	Recommended Servings
Vegetables	No limit, minimum 3.5 cups daily
Fruits	2 cups daily
Legumes	~ 3 cups weekly
Whole Grains	3 ounces daily
Fish	4 ounces 2-3x weekly
Olive oil	2 Tablespoons daily
Nuts & Seeds	Small handful ~ ¼ cup daily
Red wine	1 (4-6 oz) glass daily w/meals

MINIMIZE CONSUMPTION OF RED PROCESSED MEATS, DAIRY PRODUCTS THAT ARE HIGH IN FAT, CHIPS, REFINED GRAINS, PRODUCTS WITH ADDED SUGAR, CHIPS, FRENCH FRIES AND HIGH FRUCTOSE CORN SYRUP

Some methods for you to stay active throughout the day is to make choices that allow you to involve your body and enjoy it, such as choosing the stairs over the elevator if it is only a few floors difference, choosing to take the bike instead of the car, or walking if your destination is only a few blocks away.

Also if you are sure to eliminate calories in your diet or eating plan, as this type of diet intends, you are sure to shed some pounds. How quickly you can do this, depends on you. You really have to exercise regularly. Exercising has cardiovascular benefits and helps to reduce high blood pressure and lower bad cholesterol levels. The Mediterranean diet stays away from saturated fat, is very good for your heart and follows a healthy eating plan. It also seems to be a viable option for preventing or controlling diabetes.

A sensible plan is safe and can be fun for you to try with friends or other family members. This style of healthy eating can even get the whole family involved, though people with health conditions need to consult their doctor before making dietary changes.

Here are some benefits that can explain why it is an ideal diet to stay on.

When it comes to fat, you will stay within the official recommendation of 20 -35% of daily calories. You are keeping to the daily recommended intake of protein of 10-35%, and for carbohydrates, 50% is the ideal. It also means that you will have to use salt rarely to add flavor (preferably Mediterranean Sea Salt), and instead you will learn more about healthy cooking with these recipes and with herbs to bring out the flavor from food.

Other nutrients of concern are fiber for good digestion, potassium of sufficient amount so to counter sodium's ability to raise blood pressure and to decrease bone loss and reduce the development of kidney stones. Calcium is important to build bones and to make them stronger, and to make muscles and vessels function better. Eating yogurt, tofu, cereal and fresh fruit juice could help. Vitamin D can be had from responsible exposure to sunlight to lower the risk of bone fracture, and also getting them from low fat dairy could help. Vitamin B 12 is for better cell metabolism which can be obtained from foods that are fortified like cereal.

What makes the Mediterranean diet highly convenient when it comes to getting your daily nutritional requirement is that it involves almost all food groups. You can enjoy wine when you cook and you can plan your meals ahead, making preparation easier. It is also great to try eating al fresco and you can share your meals with loved ones and talk about the food or anything under the sun.

The fiber prescribed in this diet is enough to make you feel full and you can even indulge in fiber packed produce and whole grains. You can enjoy full taste and even add your own variant and preference.

Healthy and Powerful Tips to Easily Adopt a Mediterranean Lifestyle Now

The essential approach that you have to adopt when trying to embrace a healthier eating lifestyle for a healthier and durable weight loss is to start eating a lot more fresh green foods like vegetables, **particularly those that are grown locally and that are organic**. Red meat intake better be reduced drastically so you are on the right path to a healthier diet that will moderate the risk of heart disease and obesity problems. Also cut to the bare minimum the excessive consumption of saturated fats and transgenic fats ideally eliminating those by replacing them with healthy fats like organic olive oil and flax-seed oil. Other great substitutes for these unhealthy saturated fats that you can use are palm and coconut oils.

When this changes get implemented the results are a reduce risk of heart disease problems and many other illnesses according to many serious medical studies. An added benefit you get as the result of adopting this type of super healthy nourishment habit is that you prevent early and premature aging from occurring since your system is getting all the natural resources it needs. A vegetable based diet and a Mediterranean diet that includes recipes like the ones described in this book have tons of antioxidants, vitamins and minerals that support the fight against free radicals and early body aging signs. **The Mediterranean lifestyle embraces a slow and peaceful way of life where meals should be enjoyed with no hurry and around the congregation of friends and family**. Eating should be regarded as a peaceful and enjoyable moment in which rush has no significance.

Include Lots of Fresh Organic Veggies and Fresh Fruits in Your Meals

Get used to make fresh fruits and fresh organic veggies a frequent guest into your dinner table, this will super charge your intake of super healthy and powerful antioxidants into your diet. A true healthy Mediterranean diet is synonymous with a low-fat diet that will help you not only to control your cholesterol levels and triglycerides levels but also will lower your bad cholesterol levels (LDL). This will improve your health as the risk of fat build up inside your arteries diminishes and is greatly reduced. This obviously results in a much slighter risk of having a stroke or any heart disease related problems while you reduce obesity at the same time. Eating slow and enjoying food is part of this culture and it will help your digestive system to process all your foods in a natural and healthy way.

Make Whole Grains an Essential Part of Your Healthy Menus

Mediterranean people have the healthy habit of including wheat breads, rice, and pasta as an essential element of their menus. Rather than putting a large amount of butter onto their bread, they eat it by dipping it in delicious olive oil or a Mediterranean spicy dip.

Season Your Foods with Delicious Spices

Add flavor to your meals with delicious herbs and spices instead of salt. One particular aspect of the

Mediterranean diet is that it gives a prominent place to herbs and spices over salt so no blood pressure issues occur like when you add salt to many unhealthy recipes to enhance flavor. This habit is not only a healthier choice but also a very tasty one that gives Mediterranean food a distinctive touch of flavor.

There is a variety of spices used in the Mediterranean cuisine, and they vary according to the region. For example in the North African region of the Mediterranean spices like ginger, nutmeg, saffron, and cloves are more commonly used. In other regions, such as Southern Europe, basil, parsley, rosemary, bay laurel, and thyme are part of the cooking ingredients. As for the Eastern Mediterranean cuisine among the most commonly used spices are allspice, mint, dill, and sumac. All these spices are delicious flavor enhancers and, of course, garlic and olive oil are widely used all across. Other enhancing and delicious ingredients of this fabulous cuisine include eggplant, tomatoes, chickpeas, and lamb. Being historically a trade territory for many centuries, herbs and spices are ingredients that always have been accessible in the region and also because of a greatly fertile land these ingredients always have flourished in this part of the world.

Cook Your Meals with Healthy Unsaturated, Non-Animal Fats

Forget about unhealthy fat promoting butters or margarines and replace them with much healthier fats such as olive oil or organic canola oil. You can prevent heart disease and obesity by limiting or eliminating these types of fats from your menus. An excellent way to reduce bad cholesterol levels is by including monounsaturated fats like organic Olive oil in your menus; this is the main type of oil used for most of the best and healthiest Mediterranean recipes. Try to use **extra-virgin olive oil** so you get the most antioxidants since it gets more of them from the 1st cold pressing of the olives. It also tastes great giving a real pleasant olive flavor to your recipes.

Include Nuts in Your Healthy Mediterranean Diet

Nuts should be a part of your healthy snacks if you want to pursue the Mediterranean diet lifestyle. Nuts contain mostly unsaturated fats making them an ideal and healthy snack. Stay away from salty nuts, honey-roasted nuts and preferably consume **raw unsalted nuts**, this is better for weight loss since no added calories are present and no salt so there is no H2O retention in your body. Other nuts you can introduce into your diet are walnuts, cashews, almonds and pecans.

Limit Read Meat Consumption and Include Other Types of Meat into Your Menus

A good and healthy habit is to introduce fish twice a week into your menus. Salmon, tuna, mackerel, trout and herring are great choices to be included into your Mediterranean diet. You can eat these types of fishes in many different ways and combinations like sautéed or grilled in a slight amount of canola oil or olive oil. This constitutes an excellent source of anti-inflammatory omega-3 fatty acids and tons of healthy nutrients in your Mediterranean menus. Try to reduce the consumption of red meat to the maximum and stay away from high cholesterol foods like sausages and bacon so you stay slim and healthy.

Dairy Products

Go with low-fat cheese and low fat milk and control the consumption of these types of foods although it is quite usual to see the use of cheese in the Mediterranean menus.

If we look at the Mediterranean diet food pyramid we notice there is a difference with the usual American diet. Red meat is only consumed in small quantities and just a limited number of days during the month. More frequently you can see much more recurrent consumption of poultry, eggs and fish. Cheese and yogurt are consumed regularly. One of the top ingredients in the pyramid is olives that are consumed in big quantities. Fresh fruits and veggies can be found at the very base of this healthy Mediterranean diet pyramid. A smaller proportion is occupied by nuts and beans. Also at the base of this healthy diet you can find breads, starches pasta and grains. The Mediterranean diet is associated to a **low cholesterol diet** that is good for your hearts health and to control weight effectively. One of the reasons of this fact is that it is a low fat diet with a predominance of healthy fats like vegetable oils.

A properly balance diet of course has to include proteins and this is provided by foods like feta cheese and mozzarella cheese in the Mediterranean diet. As you put more protein into your menus more lean mass is built so more fat is burned since your metabolism increase with muscle development.

It is also interesting to notice that no sweets like sugary cakes, cadies and pastries are included as an important part of this diet so there is not an overconsumption of unnecessary calories.

Include Wine in Your Mediterranean Menus

Drinking wine in moderation is a healthy habit into the Mediterranean lifestyle. One or two glasses of wine per day are customary in this type of diet. They are usually taken accompanying meals and a good glass of wine makes every Mediterranean dish even more authentic. A good red wine is ideal to accompany the best Mediterranean recipes. Usually darker and more flavor intense wines are better to escort a good Mediterranean meal. The reason for this is that these types of wines contain **much higher levels of antioxidants and polyphenols** that will help to reduce the risks of heart diseases.

 Of course the best wines you can have are from the Mediterranean region like wines from southern France,

Sicily, Sardinia and Greece. All these wines contain high levels of **procyanadin** (powerful antioxidant substance) as well as other red wines from Australia or California. Cabernet Sauvignon wines are perfect companions of these healthy delicious recipes. Malbec wines work very good too.

There's a story in every bottle of wine.

In 1996, we planted our vineyard in the spring and later that summer, it was destroyed by a forest fire. We replanted natural rootstock cabernet sauvignon in the ashes.

2007 "Jolie" Bordeaux Style Red Wine

estate cabernet sauvignon, merlot, petit verdot, cabernet franc, *400 cases produced*

Produced and bottled by
Eden Canyon Vineyards, Creston, CA
TEL: 805.238.1241   www.edencanyon.com

CONTAINS SULFITES   14% ALC./VOL.   750ml
GOVERNMENT WARNING: (1) ACCORDING TO THE SURGEON GENERAL, WOMEN SHOULD NOT DRINK ALCOHOLIC BEVERAGES DURING PREGNANCY BECAUSE OF THE RISK OF BIRTH DEFECTS. (2) CONSUMPTION OF ALCOHOLIC BEVERAGES IMPAIRS YOUR ABILITY TO DRIVE A CAR OR OPERATE MACHINERY, AND MAY CAUSE HEALTH PROBLEMS.

Eden Canyon **http://tinyurl.com/eden-canyon**

Don´t Forget to Exercise Regularly

Make exercise a part of your daily routine and more than a routine this is a healthy habit that can be included in your Mediterranean lifestyle. Just a short walk on a regular basis is the perfect therapy for a more relaxed and a slower lifestyle where not only food is enjoyed but where the appreciation of nature is just as essential.

Avocado, fish, olive oil, canola oil and other sources of unsaturated fats are **anti-inflammatory** and fight disease right at the cellular level. **Olive oil is the best replacement for any other type of cooking oils** because of its rich unsaturated fat content and it is a **central component of the Mediterranean diet**. It could also lead to the effective prevention of obesity and other types of diabetes, creating a protective barrier combined with high proportions of plant foods, olive oil, fish and moderate consumption of red wine.

Super Healthy Mediterranean Salad with Chicken

Ingredients:

- 3/4 lb. boneless, skinless chicken breast, cut into 18 chunks

- 20 cherry tomatoes

- 1 medium organic zucchini chopped

- 1 cup of organic olives

- Large yellow pepper, cored, seeded, and cut into slices

- 1 small sweet organic onion chopped into small pieces

- 3 Tbsp. of organic balsamic vinegar

- 2 Tbsp. of Dijon mustard

- 5 Tbsp. of extra-virgin olive oil

Mediterranean Spiced Sea Salt and freshly ground organic black pepper to taste

- 1/2 a 14-ounce round whole-wheat bread loaf, cut into four slices

- 10 cups of baby organic arugula leaves, washed and spun dry

- 2 cups of organic fresh basil leaves

- 2 cups of cooked organic garbanzo beans (washed and drained if canned)

Instructions:

Use 6 bamboo skewers; thread a chunk of chicken onto one bamboo skewer, followed by a zucchini round, a cherry tomato, a pepper slice, and an organic onion chunk. This procedure has to be repeated twice so each bamboo skewer holds 3 pieces of chicken breast, 3 cherry tomatoes, 3 pepper slices, 3 zucchini slices and 3 slices of organic onions. Practice the same procedure with the other bamboo skewers.

Mix together mustard and the balsamic vinegar in a small container. Whisk in oil until this dressing gets thicker. Than season the mix with the Mediterranean Sea salt and the organic pepper. To add some flavor you can brush each bamboo skewer with two tbsp. of the vinaigrette. Use the remaining vinaigrette to season your salads. Prepare your grill grates with some oil and warm them to medium temperature.

Now once your gill grates are preheated put the skewers and cook turning them frequently every 7 to 9 minutes. Once you start to notice that vegetables and chicken turn tender you can move them to your plates. Bread has to be grilled also until it turns brown and a little crunchy. You can cut the bread in the form of croutons or little cubes or leave it into grilles slices and serve.

Distribute identical portions of the other ingredients like basil, garbanzo beans and arugula into 4 plates. Mix each salad with the croutons or the bread slices and the contained portions in 1 & 1/2 bamboo skewer, after that you can sprinkle each plate with the remaining vinaigrette. Add equal portions of organic olives to each plate.

Serves: 4

Cook Time: 20 minutes approx. total time

Super Healthy Greek Salad

Ingredients:

- 1 head of organic romaine lettuce, washed, dried and chopped
- 1 red organic onion, cut into thin slices
- 1 can pitted black olives
- 1 green bell pepper, chopped
- 1 red bell pepper, chopped
- 2 large organic tomatoes, chopped
- 1 organic cucumber, sliced
- 1 cup crumbled feta cheese
- 6 tablespoons olive oil

- 1 teaspoon dried oregano
- 1 lemon, juiced

Add ground black pepper to taste

Directions:

In a big salad container, mix the onion, the Romaine, the olives, bell peppers, tomatoes, the feta cheese and cucumber.

Mix together the oregano, the olive oil, black pepper and lemon juice. Sprinkle dressing over salad, toss and serve.

This is an amazingly delicious healthy Greek salad recipe, nice and tasty and very a very refreshing one especially for the summer time when you find lots of fresh veggies.

Serves: 6

Delicious Greek Spinach Pie – Spanakopita

This yummy Mediterranean dish belongs to the Greek cuisine. Spanakopita is a Greek pastry filled with feta cheese and delicious spinach. This wonderful recipe has an excellent taste and this combination of spinach and feta cheese with a crispy crust is just mouthwatering.

This is a Greek style delicious spinach and feta recipe wrapped in light and flaky golden brown fillow dough. This pie is full of pleasant fresh herbs that make it truly a unique Mediterranean recipe to be enjoyed at any time.

Servings: makes 4 servings

Prep Time: 20 minutes

Cook Time: 40 minutes

Total Time: 1 hour

Ingredients:

- 2 pounds of organic spinach, steamed, squeezed, drained and chopped
- 1 cup feta, crumbled
- 1/4 cup dill, chopped
- 1/4 cup parsley, chopped
- 1/4 cup of organic green onions, sliced
- 3 eggs, lightly beaten
- Mediterranean Sea Salt and pepper to taste
- 1/4 cup extra virgin olive oil
- 12 sheets fillow dough

Directions:

Mingle the spinach, parsley, feta cheese, eggs, dill, green onions, sea salt and pepper in a big container.

Use pastry brush to paint a layer of extra virgin olive oil into the bottom of an 8x8 inch baking pan.

Brush the top of a sheet of fillow dough with extra virgin olive oil and place it in the pan. (If the fillow dough doesn´t fit the pan then you have to cut it.) Repeat this process until you obtain six layers.

Place the organic spinach mixture on top of the fillow dough.

Brush the top of a sheet of fillow dough with extra virgin olive oil and place it on the spinach. Repeat this procedure until you have six layers.

Now it is ready to be baked in a preheated 350F oven until it turns golden brown on top, approx. 30-50 minutes.

Delicious Mallorcan Eggplant Bake – Tumbet Mallorquin

This is a super healthy vegetarian recipe originally from the island of Mallorca in Spain in the Mediterranean Sea. This yummy and traditional dish is filled with amazing ingredients like zucchini, eggplants, garlic, delicious tomato sauce and potatoes. This marvelous healthy recipe can be supplemented with fish, eggs or lamb for added protein; this is an ideal light meal to be enjoyed at any time.

Preparation Time: 10 minutes

Cook Time: 40 minutes

Total Time: 50 minutes

Yield: 4 Servings

Ingredients:

- 3 Japanese eggplants
- 1 cup (250 ml) olive oil
- 4 large potatoes (1.5 lbs)
- 2 medium zucchini
- 4 cloves garlic
- 1 (28 oz) can crushed tomatoes

Mediterranean Sea salt and pepper to taste

Method:

Cut eggplants into slices. Also cut potatoes into thin slices and salt them. Cut zucchini into thin slices. Peel the garlic and chop it with energy.

Warm the olive oil in a <u>heavy cast-iron frying skillet</u>. Hit the pan and then add some olive oil and heat on medium. When has reached a high temperature then fry eggplant slices lightly. Drain the eggplant slices using a paper towel.

The next step is to fry the sliced potatoes until golden. Next you can move the potatoes to a casserole plate. Place eggplant slices on top of potatoes.

Lightly fry the zucchini into hot oil. Drain with paper towels after removing. Now you can place it on top of the eggplants.

Get rid of almost all the remaining oil and just keep a small amount of it into the cooking pan. Then lightly fry the chopped garlic in the remaining oil. Mix with the crushed tomatoes just before garlic turns golden and stir for five minutes approximately. The final step is to pour the tomato sauce over the top of the veggies and serve cold or hot.

Delicious Tuna Farfalle a la Puttanesca

Ingredients:

- 2 (5 ounce) cans tuna, drained and flaked (Bumble Bee)
- 1 lb dry farfalle pasta or 1 lb bow tie pasta
- 4 tablespoons olive oil
- 3 garlic cloves, minced
- 2 medium onions cut in 1/4 inch slices
- 1 (14 1/2 ounce) can diced tomatoes with juice
- 1 cup dry white wine
- 3 tablespoons capers, drained
- 1 tablespoon chopped rosemary

- 1/2 cup kalamata olive, pitted and cut in quarters
- 1 teaspoon ground black pepper
- Mediterranean Sea salt
- 2 tablespoons chopped Italian parsley

Method:

I - Cook the pasta according to your taste or package directions

II - Set aside.

III - Place oil in a large cooking pan over medium heat.

IV - Add organic onions organic garlic and sauté for about five minutes. Add rosemary, tomatoes and juice, capers, wine, rosemary, pepper and olives to onions.

V - Cook for approximately five minutes.

VI - Raise heat to medium and heat for an additional three minutes until the sauce gets a thicker consistency.

VII - Add Mediterranean Sea salt to taste.

VII - Mix the pasta with the tuna and parsley.

This healthy Mediterranean Recipe is just 520 calories approx. based on an individual serving size of 300 g. This recipe serves 6

Delicious Stuffed Chicken Breasts with Spinach

If Spanakopita (Greek spinach pie) is one of your favorites then you will love this delicious stuffed chicken recipe. This recipe includes a yummy and healthy spinach pie filling stuffed inside a chicken breast; you can enjoy this wonderful Mediterranean dish baked to perfection!

Spinach and Feta Stuffed Chicken Breasts

Servings: 4

- Serving Size: two pieces

Approximately Calories: 205

Approx. Fat: 3.8 g

Approx. Protein: 35.0 g

Approx. Carbs: 10.5 g

Approx. Fiber Content: 2.7 g

Ingredients:

- 10 oz package frozen chopped spinach, thawed & juice squeezed out
- 1 tsp. of extra virgin olive oil
- 1/2 cup (2.5 oz.) fat free Feta cheese
- 1/3 cup fat free ricotta
- 1/4 cup chopped parsley
- 1/4 cup chopped scallions
- 1/2 onion, chopped
- 2 cloves garlic

- Mediterranean Sea Salt and pepper
- 3 (1.25 lbs.) chicken breast halves
- 1 egg
- 1 tbsp. of pure water
- 1/2 cup whole wheat seasoned breadcrumbs (I used 4C)
- Spray oil

Toothpicks

In a small sauté cast iron skillet, heat oil. Add onions, scallions, garlic and sauté about one minute. Add organic spinach and organic parsley, Mediterranean Sea salt and pepper and cook for one more minute. Move away from heat, add ricotta cheese and feta.

Preheat oven to 350°.

Now slice chicken breast halves into three thin cutlets. Make the chicken breast halves thinner by pounding them. This step will help to wrap the cutlets. Season the chicken with Mediterranean Sea salt and pepper.

Place approximately 1/4 cup of spinach mixture in the center of the chicken. Roll it and secure the ends with toothpicks to avoid filling from coming out. It is just fine if is not perfect. The egg wash and bread crumbs will keep everything in place.

Dip the chicken cuts into egg wash, then breadcrumbs.

Spray a cookie sheet with oil and place chicken on cookie sheet. Lightly spray the chicken cuts with oil and bake approximately for 30 minutes, until cooked through. Eliminate the toothpicks and serve.

Makes 9 pieces

Delicious Mediterranean Herb Shrimp with Penne

Serves: 6

Preparation Time: 5 minutes

Cook Time: 15 minutes

Ingredients:

- 8 ounces of penne pasta

- 1   lb.   large shrimp, peeled and deveined

- 2   c   fresh or frozen small broccoli florets

- 1   c   fat free half-and-half

- 4   oz.   Neufchátel cheese (1/3 less fat than cream cheese), cubed

- 2   t   McCormick® Perfect Pinch® <u>Mediterranean Herb Seasoning</u>

- 1⁄2 t   Mediterranean Sea Salt

            Grated Parmesan or Asiago cheese (optional)

Method:

1. Cook pasta in large pan as directed on package, adding shrimp and broccoli during the last three minutes of cooking. Drain well.

2. Meanwhile, bring half-and-half to simmer in small saucepan on medium heat. Reduce heat to medium-low. Add cream cheese, Seasoning and Mediterranean Sea salt; whisk until cheese is melted and sauce is well mixed.

3. Place pasta, shrimp and broccoli in serving bowl. Add sauce; toss gently to coat well. If you want you can

sprinkle with Parmesan cheese (completely optional). Now it is ready to serve!

This marvelous healthy recipe is simple to make and it is just 260 calories approximately per serving. One of the great advantages of the Mediterranean diet is that it lets you consume the right amount of healthy carbs so that your metabolism doesn't slows down.

Delicious Mediterranean Grilled Salmon

This is a really fast and super healthy recipe made with salmon including Mediterranean spices and ingredients. I am sure you will love this one! Enjoy!

Ingredients:

- 1/2 cup olive oil
- 1/4 cup balsamic vinegar
- 4 cloves garlic, pressed
- 4 (3 ounce) fillets salmon

- 1 tablespoon chopped fresh cilantro
- 1 tablespoon chopped fresh basil
- 1 1/2 teaspoons garlic salt

Method:

The balsamic oil and vinegar have to be mingled together in a small container. Display the salmon fillets in a shallow baking dish. Brush garlic onto the fillets, after that pour the oil and vinegar over them, turning once to coat. You can spice it up with cilantro, garlic, basil, and Mediterranean Sea salt. Set apart to marinate for ten minutes.

Preheat your oven's broiler to 350 degrees *Cook 10-12 mins*

Arrange the salmon approximately 6 inches from the heat source, and broil for 15 minutes, turning once, or until golden browned on both sides and easily flaked with a fork. Sporadically brush the salmon with the sauce from the pan. *Longer than 15 mins. will make the fish tough*

Approximately preparation time: 10 minutes

Approx. cooking time: 15 minutes

Delicious and Healthy Mediterranean Grilled Chicken Kebabs

This is a delicious and healthy recipe of kebabs that can be dipped in the dressing leftover. It can be deliciously and tastefully be enhanced with fresh pomegranate seeds. This tasty recipe is very low in calories and can be enjoyed any time during the week.

Ingredients:

- 1 cup Pomegranate-Orange Dressing, divided
- 2 pounds skinless, boneless chicken thighs, trimmed and cut into bite-sized pieces $
- 2 large oranges
- 1/4 teaspoon salt
- 1/4 teaspoon freshly ground black pepper $
- Cooking spray $
- 1/4 cup chopped fresh mint

Preparation:

Start by mixing 1/2 cup Pomegranate-Orange Dressing (or balsamic vinegar) and chicken in a large zip-top plastic bag. Seal and marinate in refrigerator for about 30 minutes, rotating the plastic bag occasionally.

Prepare grill to medium-high heat.

Cut each orange into 8 slices; cut each slice crosswise into 3 pieces.

Take away chicken from marinade; discard marinade. Thread orange and chicken pieces alternately onto each of 16 (10-inch) skewers. Sprinkle uniformly with salt and pepper. Arrange the chicken kebabs on a grill rack coated with cooking spray; grill for 5 minutes approximately on each side or until chicken is done, moist occasionally with

remaining 1/2 cup Pomegranate-Orange Dressing.
Arrange the chicken kebabs on a plate; sprinkle with mint.

Delicious Grouper with Tomato & Olive Sauce

Note: this type of white-fleshed fish can be enjoyed in many ways; it can be steamed, broiled, grilled, baked or poached. It is full of vitamins and minerals like potassium, iron, B vitamins and an excellent source of protein.

Ingredients:

- 4 grouper fillets or steaks, each 5 ounces and about 1-inch thick
- 1/2 teaspoon salt

- 1/4 teaspoon freshly ground black pepper
- 1 1/2 tablespoons extra-virgin olive oil
- 1 yellow onion, finely chopped
- 2 cloves garlic, minced
- 3 tomatoes, peeled and seeded, then diced
- 5 large pimiento-stuffed green olives, sliced
- 1 tablespoon capers, rinsed
- 1 jalapeno chili, seeded and cut into 1-inch julienne
- 2 tablespoons fresh lime juice

Method:

You can now sprinkle the both sides of the grouper steaks with 1/4 teaspoon of the Mediterranean Sea salt and 1/8 teaspoon of pepper. Use a large, nonstick frying pan to heat 1 1/2 teaspoons of the olive oil over medium-high heat. Put the fish on the pan and sear on both sides until lightly browned, approximately two minutes a side. Arrange on a plate and keep warm.

After that you can now add 1 tbsp. of the remaining olive oil into the pan and ease the temperature to medium heat. Add the onion and sauté until soft and lightly golden, approx. 6 minutes. Add the garlic and sauté until softened, approx. 1 minute. Add the tomatoes, capers, olives, jalapeno and capersand simmer for 10 minutes to allow the flavors to mix. Whisk the remaining 1/4 teaspoon salt and 1/8 teaspoon pepper. Put back the fish to the pan, cover and cook until the fish turns golden brown all over and consistent when tested with the tip of a knife, approx. six to eight minutes.

Arrange the grouper steaks to warmed separate platters. Pour the lime juice into the vegetables and pan juices and serve some sauce over each steak.

Now it's ready to be served! Enjoy!

This super healthy recipe is just under 220 calories and low fat with lots of protein.

Serves 4

Delicious and Healthy Polenta with Mediterranean Veggies

The best way to prepare this recipe is to have all your veggies ready and cut the day before and store them refrigerated into a container. It is a good idea to roast all the veggies, zucchini, eggplant, red pepper and mushrooms in the morning and keep them refrigerated until you need to use them for this recipe.

Ingredients:

- 1 small eggplant, peeled, cut into 1/4-inch slices
- 1 small yellow zucchini, cut into 1/4-inch slices
- 1 small green zucchini, cut into 1/4-inch slices
- 6 medium mushrooms, sliced
- 1 sweet red pepper, seeded, cored and cut into chunks
- 2 tablespoons plus 1 teaspoon extra-virgin olive oil
- 6 cups water
- 1 1/2 cups coarse polenta (corn grits)
- 2 teaspoons trans-free margarine
- 1/4 teaspoon cracked black pepper
- 10 ounces frozen spinach, thawed
- 2 plum (Roma) tomatoes, sliced
- 6 dry-packed sun-dried tomatoes, soaked in water to rehydrate, drained and chopped
- 10 ripe olives, chopped
- 2 teaspoons oregano

Method:

Heat the broiler (grill). Position the rack approximately four inches from the heat source.

Brush the eggplant, mushrooms, red pepper and zucchini with 1 tbsp. of the olive oil. Place in a single layer on a baking sheet and broil under low heat. Turn as required and sporadically brush with 1 tbsp. of olive oil. When it turns tender and somewhat browned, take away from the broiler. Use immediately or cover and refrigerate for future use.

Now preheat the oven to 350 F. Coat a decorative, ovenproof 12-inch flan or quiche dish with cooking spray.

In a medium size pan, boil water. Reduce heat and gradually whisk in polenta. Continue to stir and cook for approx. 5 minutes. When polenta comes away from side of pan, stir in margarine and spice with 1/8 teaspoon of the black pepper. Take away from heat.

Spread polenta into the base and sides of the baking bowl. Brush with one teaspoon of olive oil. Place in the oven and bake for 10 minutes. Remove and keep warm.

Drain spinach and press between paper towels. Top polenta with spinach. Arrange a layer of sliced tomatoes, chopped sun-dried tomatoes and olives. Top with remaining roasted vegetables. Sprinkle with oregano and the remaining 1/8 teaspoon black pepper. Return to the oven for another 10 minutes. When warmed through, remove from the oven. Cut into 6 wedges and serve.

Serves 6

This healthy Mediterranean Recipe is just under 250 calories and low fat.

Delicious Spinach and Feta Pita Bake

Serves: 6

Ingredients:

- 6 whole wheat pita breads, each 6'' wide
- 2 roma tomatoes, chopped
- 4 fresh mushrooms, sliced

- One bunch spinach, washed and chopped
- 2 tbsp. Parmesan cheese, grated
- ½ cup feta cheese, crumbled
- 1 can (6 oz) sun-dried tomato pesto
- Pinch of ground black pepper
- 1 cup of olives
- 3 tbsp. olive oil

Method:

- Warm up your oven to 350 degrees F.
- Place a small portion of tomato pesto onto one of the pita bread and spread it all evenly over it on one side.
- Arrange them onto a baking sheet, with the pesto side facing up and scatter the chopped tomatoes on top.
- Spread the spinach over the tomatoes and top it up with layers of mushrooms, olives and feta cheese.
- Sprinkle the grated parmesan cheese on top and smother the topping with a lashing of olive oil.
- Season with a dash of ground black pepper and place in the hot oven.
- Cook for about 12 minutes or until the edges of the pita breads turn crispy and the veggies roast.
- Remove from oven and slice it into wedges.

Serve right away and enjoy!

Delicious Classic Greek Moussaka with Eggplant

Moussaka (moo-sah-KAH) is possibly one of the best known and renowned Greek dishes.

This formula is a product of playing with the customary ingredients to come up with a lighter and healthier vegetarian moussaka formula. The preparation of this particular recipe requires some time so it is not the best recipe to be looking at if you are in a hurry, but it is worth the wait believe me, it is just delicious! When you have the luxury of time to dedicate to arrange the vegetables and baking the dish, it will make a fabulous dinner entree for your friends and family alike.

Prep Time: one hour, 15 minutes

Cook Time: 45 minutes

Total Time: 2 hours

Ingredients:

- 2-3 eggplants (about 1 1/2 pounds), sliced lengthwise in 1/4 inch slices
- 1 1/2 pounds zucchini, sliced lengthwise in 1/4 inch slices
- 1 1/4 pounds potatoes
- 2 cups breadcrumbs
- 4 eggs, separated (reserve yolks for Bechamel)
- 2 tbsp. olive oil
- 1 medium onion, diced

- 2 garlic cloves, minced
- 1 15 oz. can chickpeas, (Garbanzo) drained, rinsed, and mashed
- 1 15 oz. can diced tomatoes, with liquid
- 2 tbsp. tomato paste
- 1/4 tsp. ground cinnamon
- 1 tsp. dried oregano
- 1/2 tsp. ground cumin
- 1 tsp. sugar
- Salt and pepper to taste
- 3/4 cup grated Kefalotyri or Parmesan cheese

Bechamel Sauce:

- 1/2 cup butter (1 stick)
- 1/2 cup flour
- 3 cups milk, warmed
- 4 egg yolks (reserved from above)
- A pinch of ground nutmeg

Method:

Preheat the oven to 400 degrees.

Arrange the vegetables:

Arrange the zucchini and eggplant slices in a colander and salt them generously. Cover with an inverted bowl weighted down by a heavy container or pot. Place the colander in the sink so that the extra moisture can be drawn out. They will need to sit for approximately 15to 20 minutes

Peel the potatoes and boil them whole for approx. 10 minutes. The consistency should be just tender and not too soft. Drain, cool, and slice them in 1/4 inch slices. Set apart.

Cover a baking sheet with aluminum foil and lightly grease. Add some drops of water to the egg whites and beat lightly with a fork or whisk. Spread breadcrumbs on a plane platter.

Rinse the zucchini and eggplant slices and blot the additional moisture with paper towels. Arrange the zucchini away with the potatoes. Dip the eggplant wedges in the beaten egg whites and then dredge them in the breadcrumbs, coating both sides. Arrange breaded eggplant wedges on the baking sheet and bake for 30 minutes, turning them one time throughout cooking.

When eggplant has completed cooking, lower the oven temperature to 350 degrees.

Tomato Sauce Preparation:

Heat the olive oil in a big saute pan. Add onion and saute until translucent, approx. five minutes. Add garlic and heat until fragrant, approx. 1 minute. Add mashed chickpeas to pan with tomatoes, cumin, cinnamon, tomato paste, pepper sugar, Mediterranean Sea salt, and oregano. Allow the sauce to simmer uncovered so that extra liquid can be cooked out.

Prepare the Moussaka:

Lightly grease a 9 x 13 x 3 inch baking pan. Sprinkle the bottom of the pan with breadcrumbs. Cover the bottom of the pan with a layer of potatoes by leaving a tiny space nearby the edges. Top with a layer of eggplant wedges. Add tomato sauce on top of eggplant and sprinkle with grated cheese. Add zucchini wedges next. Top with another layer of eggplant wedges and sprinkle once again with grated cheese.

Prepare the Bechamel Sauce:

Dissolve butter over low heat. Using a whisk, add flour to liquefied butter constantly stirring to make a smooth paste. Allow the flour to cook for 60 seconds but avoid for it to be brown.

Add warmed milk to this mix in a balanced stream, constantly stirring.

Cook over low heat until it thickens a bit but does not boil. Take away from heat, and stir in beaten egg yolks and pinch of nutmeg. Put back into heat and mix until sauce thickens, being careful not to burn it.

Prepared for Oven:

Pour in the béchamel sauce over the eggplant and be sure to let sauce to load the sides and corners of the pan. Smooth the béchamel on top with a knife and sprinkle with the left over grated cheese. Bake in 350 degree oven for 45 minutes or until béchamel sauce is a pleasant golden brown color. Allow to cool for approx. 15 to 20 minutes before serving and sharing.

You can prepare this recipe ahead up until the making of the béchamel sauce and refrigerate. Prepare the béchamel sauce just before you expect to bake it.

Delicious and Healthy Pasta Cannelini

This DELICIOUS and low calorie pasta recipe entree features a fresh-tasting tomato accompanied with white bean sauce. Serve it with a tossed salad or with fresh steamed vegetables.

Ingredients: (Serves 4. Each 1-1/2 cup serving)

- two cups dry penne pasta
- 1/2 teaspoon minced organic garlic

- 1/2 organic sliced onion
- 1/2 red sliced bell pepper
- two cups pasta sauce
- 1/2 cup of pure water
- 15 oz. can white rinsed and drained cannellini beans
- 1/2 teaspoon dried oregano
- 1 cup of organic baby tomatoes

Method: (Ready in approx. 20 Minutes)

1. Cook the pasta according to the package directions (*).

2. In a colander drain the pasta

3. Spray a big, nonstick frying pan with extra virgin olive oil cooking spray and heat over medium-high heat.

4. Saute the garlic until lightly golden. Add the remaining ingredients and bring to a boil.

5. Cook until the onions and the tomatoes have a tender consistency. Mix the pasta with the sauce.

6. Sprinkle some mint leaves and feta cheese over each plate

(*) To make this healthy recipe a much better choice for your weight loss diet you can reduce the glycemic index of the pasta by cooking it "al dente" or to the teeth. This is a very fast and easy to prepare delicious Mediterranean dish. Check the consistency of the pasta after approx. 7 minutes of being cooked and look for a small resistance in the middle of it when you chew it. Keep on trying until you reach "al dente" consistency.

Nutritional Information per Serving:

Cal: 270 approx.

Fat: 1.5 g

Sat. Fat: 0 g

Cholesterol: 0 mg

Carbs: 53 g

Sugars: 8.7 g

Sodium: 400 mg

Protein: 12 g

Fiber: 6 g

YOUR NOTES

Delicious Mediterranean Stuffed Tomatoes

These delicious stuffed tomatoes can be served as a main meal or as a side dish and they are very easy to prepare. They can be enjoyed and served at room temperature and it makes a wonderful dish for a warm summer day. Your dinner table is going to look just fantastic with this very appealing presentation of fresh stuffed tomatoes in Mediterranean Style. This is of course a very healthy meal that can be enjoyed any time during the week, low in calories and full of antioxidants

Ingredients:

-   2 quarts of pure water

- 1 1/2 cups raw orzo pasta
- PESTO
- 1 1/2 cups fresh basil leaves, packed
- 2 garlic cloves, minced (or pressed)
- 1/4 cup pistachio nut
- 1/2 cup grated parmesan cheese
- 1/4 cup olive oil
- salt & freshly ground black pepper
- 1 teaspoon olive oil
- 6 large ripe tomatoes
- 1 dash salt & fresh ground pepper
- 1/3 cup tiny cubes feta cheese
- 1/2 cup chopped kalamata olive
- chopped fresh basil (to garnish)

Method:

1. Boil water in a large container. Add the orzo, stir, lower the heat, cover, and simmer for approx. 7 minutes, stirring as required.

2. Mix the basil leaves, garlic, pistachios and parmesan in a food processor while the orzo cooks. Whirl until well sliced.

3. Add the olive oil over the hopper in a thin stream to make a soft paste, stopping to scrape down the sides a twice as needed.

4. Spice it up to taste with Mediterranean Sea salt and pepper.

5. Drain the orzo. Toss it gently with the teaspoon of olive oil and let it turn cooler to room temperature.

6. With a sharp serrated knife, cut a portion of approximately two inched across in the top of each tomato and get rid of the core. Scoop out the pulp with a small spoon or melon baller, leaving a 1/2 inch thick shell.

7. Gently sprinkle the insides of the tomatoes with Mediterranean Sea salt and pepper.

8. Mingle the cooled orzo with the Pesto and feta cheese cubes. Taste for flavor and tweak as required.

9. Stuff each one of the tomatoes with approx. one cup of the filling.

10. Sprinkle the tops with the olives and garnish with the chopped basil.

This healthy recipe has just 379 calories per serving approximately and 4,5 g of fiber approx.

Serves 6

Delicious Rissoto with Salmon & Asparagus

Ingrediets:

- 1 diced medium onion (approximately 1 cup)
- 4 tablespoons butter
- 1 lemon
- 1 cup arborio rice
- 2 cups chicken broth
- 2 cups water
- 8 to 12 spears cooked asparagus, cut into 1-inch lengths approx.
- 8 ounces salmon filet, skin and bones removed and cut into 1-inch pieces
- 3/4 cup grated parmesan cheese
- Extra parmesan to garnish each dish

Method:

1. Stew the onion in butter over medium heat until soft, then zest the lemon and stir it with the onion.

2. Stir in the rice to coat all the grains of rice with butter.

3. Start adding broth 1/2 cup at a time. Adjust the heat so the broth just simmers. The broth will decrease and begin to have a gel consistency. When it thickens add more pure water by adding ½ a cup each time. Stir regularly and go on until the rice is almost done. In the meantime, squeeze the lemon and add a couple tablespoons along with some broth. (Save the remaining of lemon juice to season the dish with at the end.)

- Slice the asparagus and salmon into 1-inch pieces.

4. When the rice is just a tad underdone, stir in the parmesan cheese. Spice it up with Mediterranean Sea salt, pepper, and lemon juice. Let it rest hot, then...

5. Take away the pan from the heat and stir in the asparagus and salmon. Cover the pot and let it rest for five minutes approx. Now the salmon should be generally cooked, but it may need a few seconds more. Serve with grated or shaved parmesan over the top. (Don't stir too much or you'll break up the fish.)

Delicious and Healthy Seafood Paella

This is a gorgeous dish full of nutrients.

Ingredients (Serves 4)

- 400 g risotto or long-grain rice
- 600 ml vegetable stock
- 1 medium onion, finely chopped
- 2 garlic cloves, finely chopped
- 50 g sun dried tomatoes
- 40 g mushrooms, sliced
- 2 baby courgettes, sliced
- ½ tsp saffron

- 2 tbsp garden peas
- 6 small broccoli florets
- 100 g large uncooked prawns, shelled
- 100 g salmon fillet
- 1 tbsp extra virgin olive oil

- 1 tbsp water

Method:

1. Put the rice and stock together in a large pan and bring to the boil. Sprinkle in saffron and simmer until rice is cooked. Drain.

2. Fry the salmon in the oil until lightly browned add the prawns and cook a few additional minutes. Take away the seafood, and then cut the salmon.

3. Fry the onion, garlic, mushroom, and courgette until lightly browned. Pour in water. Once it sizzles, add remaining vegetables. Stir-fry for approx. 10 minutes, then fold in the rice and seafood and serve.

Delicious Homemade Mediterranean Pizza

Ingredients:

- 1 cup warm water
- 1 package active dry yeast
- 1 ½ cups unbleached all-purpose flour
- 1 cup whole wheat flour
- 2 tbsp. olive oil
- ½ tsp. salt
- 1 tbsp. honey
- 1 cup chopped tomatoes

- 4 chopped dried figs
- ½ cup shredded Prosciutto
- ¼ cup finely grated Parmesan
- ¼ cup fresh mozzarella
- ½ cup crumbled Gorgonzola
- Sprinkled rosemary
- Sprinkled garlic

Method:

1. Mix the water, yeast, and all-purpose flour in a large dish and combine together. Add the olive oil and salt, and slowly add the whole wheat flour to the bowl. Work the components together until the dough holds its shape.

2. Place the dough on a lightly floured surface and knead until elastic (approximately five minutes).

Move the dough to a lightly oiled dish and cover with a towel. Let it rest for one hour approximately (or until dough has doubled in size).

3. When risen, arrange the dough back on the lightly floured surface; divide the dough and roll into balls. Cover the dough with a towel again and let it rest for another 15 – 20 minutes approx.

4. Shape the dough and preheat the oven to 500 degrees. Place the two pieces of dough on a pizza stone lightly covered with oil and cornmeal.

5. Sprinkle on the tomatoes, followed by the gorgonzola, mozzarella, prosciutto and parmesan, then top with rosemary, figs and garlic. Place inside the oven and bake for approx. 20 minutes or until lightly browned

You can combine the sweet with the salty whenever you are undecided which way to go when it comes to satisfy your cravings.

This marvelous homemade Mediterranean dish will certainly satisfy all your cravings with a unique and fresh flavor that combines the sweet with the salty flavors in an amazing and delicious fusion. Enjoy!

You'll be transported to the Italian countryside once you enjoy this homemade pizza. Top a gently honeyed wheat crust with loud zests and flavors of gorgonzola, rosemary, figs and prosciutto. This makes a wonderful and delicious meal to be enjoyed any time during the week.

This marvelous homemade creation is a perfect excuse to gather with your family members or friends and enjoy a Mediterranean lifestyle and share a cup of red wine. So just plan your next family dinner and enjoy this recipe with your loved ones!

Delicious Mediterranean Style Spaghetti with Clams

Serves 4

An essential component of this classic Mediterranean meal is lemon. Try to use only small clams for this dish and be careful not to ruin them by overcooking.

Ingredients:

- 1/2 cup extra-virgin olive oil
- 8 garlic cloves, thinly sliced
- 3 pounds fresh Manila clams or small littleneck clams, scrubbed
- 1/4 cup plus 2 tablespoons chopped fresh Italian parsley
- 1/2 cup dry white wine
- 1/4 cup fresh lemon juice
- 1 pound spaghetti

Method:

Heat the oil in a large pan over medium-high heat. Add sliced garlic and sauté until light brown, approx. one minute. Add clams and 1/4 cup chopped Italian parsley; stir for about 2 minutes. Add wine; simmer for about 2 minutes. Add fresh lemon juice. Cover and simmer until clams open; approx. 6 minutes (get rid of any clams that do not open).

In the meantime, cook pasta in large pot of boiling salted water until just tender but still firm to bite (al dente). Drain. Add pasta to calm mixture and toss to coat. Add some flavor with Mediterranean Sea salt and pepper. Move to large bowl. Sprinkle with remaining 2 tbsp. of parsley and serve.

YOUR NOTES

Delicious and Healthy Mediterranean Style Baked Salmon

Ingredients:

- 1 cup diced tomato
- 3 tablespoons olive oil

- 1 tablespoon red wine vinegar
- 1/2 cup chopped Greek extra virgin olive oil
- 1/4 cup diced red onion
- 2 tablespoons capers
- 2 chopped garlic cloves
- 1/2 teaspoon salt
- 1/4 teaspoon pepper
- 1 lb. salmon fillet

Method:

1. Mix first 8 ingredients.
2. Spread mixture over salmon.
3. Bake at 350 for 30 minutes.

Total cooking and preparation time: 45 minutes

This is a low calorie healthy recipe with just 265 calories per serving approx.

Serves 4

Delicious Risotto with Salmon and Green Peppers

Ingredients:

- 2 fresh salmon (fillets)
- 3 oz. shrimp (prawns)
- 1 vegetable stock (cube)
- 5 oz. risotto rice

- 1 pt. boiling water
- 2 bay leaves
- 2 tbsps. crème fraiche (cream)
- 2 tsps. dill (dried)
- 1 tsp. herbs (dried)
- 1 lemon juice (approx.)
- lemon zest
- olive oil
- Mediterranean Sea salt
- pepper

Method:

1. Heat 1 tbsp. of olive oil in a pan; add dried herbs, bay leaf and risotto rice when hot. Continue to stir for 5 minutes.

2. Make up stock and eliminate salmon skin/bone.

3. Add 1/3 stock to rice after 5 minutes, add the rest of it until it is all absorbed (approx. 10-15 minutes). Stir regularly.

4. While risotto is cooking, add 1 tbsp. olive oil, lemon zest, crème fraiche and dill to hot frying pan. Wait until simmering, DO NOT BOIL.

5. Add salmon to frying pan and fry. This will take approximately 5 to 8 minutes; turn two times until flakey and soft.

6. Add lemon juice, twist of black pepper and pinch of Mediterranean Sea salt to risotto, add shrimps and simmer for another five minutes.

7. Lightly break up salmon into flakes using a wooden spoon, and add to risotto. Remove bay leaves.

8. Serve hot. Garnish with lemon rind/bay leaf.

Approx. calories: 580

Total cooking time: 30 minutes

Delicious Mediterranean Veggie Lasagna

This is a yummy Mediterranean recipe filled with veggies and excellent to be served and shared with friends and family.

Ingredients:

- 1 1/2 tbsp. of extra virgin olive oil
- 1 (10 oz.) package frozen artichoke hearts, thawed and sliced
- 2 (14 oz.) cans black olives, halved
- 1 chopped red organic onion
- 3 stalks of chopped celery

- 10 sliced green onions
- 2 small chopped zucchini
- 1 large roasted red pepper, diced
- 1 (10 oz.) package frozen spinach, thawed
- 2 tbsp. of fresh chopped garlic
- 2 lbs. asparagus, trimmed and chopped into 1/2 inch pieces
- 10 oz. sun-dried tomatoes packed in oil, drained and diced
- 3 tbsp. of fresh chopped sweet basil
- 15 lasagna noodles, cooked according to package instructions
- 8 oz. of parmesan asiago cheese, shredded (or feta if you would desire)
- 6 tbsp. butter
- 1/2 cup flour
- 5 cups milk

Method:

1. Preheat oven to 375 degrees F.

2. Heat oil in a large pot over medium-high heat.

3. Add red organic onion, organic green onion, garlic and organic celery.

4. Saute till onion is translucent and celery starts to soften.

5. Add the other vegetables, one at a time, stirring before adding each one.

6. Cover and cook 5 minutes, stirring one time.

7. Uncover and cook until veggies are tender, stirring often, approx. 10 minutes longer.

8. Spice it up with Mediterranean Sea salt and pepper.

9. Melt butter in large sauce pan over medium heat.

10. Whisk in flour.

11. Whisk 2 minutes.

12. Slowly whisk in milk.

13. Cook until mixture comes to a boil, whisking often.

14. Remove from heat and season with salt and pepper.

15. Spoon 1 cup of sauce over bottom of your lasagna pan.

16. Place 5 lasagna noodles atop sauce, overlapping slightly.

17. Spoon 1/2 of veggies over noodles.

18. Spoon 1 1/2 cups sauce over veggies.

19. Sprinkle 1/3 of your cheese over sauce.

20. Replicate each layer once.

21. Top with the last 5 lasagna noodles.

22. Spoon remaining sauce over noodles.

23. Top with remaining cheese.

24. You can now refrigerate for future use, just cover firmly.

25. Bake Lasagna uncovered on center rack until sauce is bubbling, approx. 40 minutes, 55 minutes if chilled before.

26. Remove from oven and allow to stand for approx. 10-15 minutes before cutting and serving.

Total preparation time: 1 hour and 30 minutes

Delicious Homemade Tomato Sauce

Ingredients:

- 10 large ripe tomatoes (choose instead 30 Roma tomatoes since they are easier to peel and you can squeeze the seeds with no trouble)
- 2 tbsp. olive oil
- 2 tbsp. of light butter
- 1 white chopped onion
- 1 large green bell pepper chopped
- 2 organic carrots scraped and chopped
- 6 minced organic garlic cloves
- 1/4 cup chopped fresh basil (Prefer Greek basil)
- 1 tbsp. of Italian seasoning

- 2 tbsp. of finely chopped fresh organic oregano
- 1 cup Burgundy wine (or any other red wine you like)
- 2 bay leaves
- 2 stalks of organic celery
- 6 ounces tomato paste (You can use canned or prepare your own if you have a lot of time and patience)
- Mediterranean Sea salt and pepper

Method:

1. Put water to boil in a big container. Have a big bowl of cold water with ice ready. Drop whole tomatoes into the boiling water, preferably rolling them inside so you avoid splashing, approx. for 1 min. Remove with slotted spoon and place in the ice water bath. Let the tomatoes rest in the water till they cool down sufficiently to be manipulated again. After that remove the peel and get rid of the seeds. Mix the tomatoes in food processor or a blender. If you want a "chunky" consistence for your sauce then chop 2 or 3 of the tomatoes and set apart.

2. Use a big pot oven to cook onion, garlic, carrot and bell pepper, and in oil and low fat butter until onion starts to become softer, approximately for 5 minutes (over medium heat). Pour in pureed tomatoes. Stir in chopped

Italian seasoning, oregano, tomato, basil, oregano and wine. Arrange bay leaf and whole celery stalks in the pot. Bring to a boil, then decrease heat to low, cover and simmer for approx. two hours. Stir in the tomato paste and simmer another two hours (the consistency of each lot of sauce may change contingent to multiple factors). Your taste in the sauce thickness will determine how you adjust the temperature and the simmering up or down. Remove celery and bay leaf.

4. Now you can smooth the sauce by using the food processor once again or the blender, it depends on your taste and how you like your sauce consistency. With this step your sauce is ready to be used in multiple different recipes and you can thicken the sauce once again by adding more chopped vegetables so it gets chunky again.

5. Sauce Storage: This sauce can be stored for about 2 weeks while refrigerated although given the large batch it makes you probably want to be able to store it for longer periods of time. So a good alternative is to freeze the sauce using some sort of plastic containers. Glass would be ideal but it cracks with extreme cold temperatures so plastic is a god alternative in this case.

6. I also can my tomato sauce by processing it in canning jars and a hot water bath. The Internet is full of canning instructions if you decide to can.

However, once you open a jar of the canned sauce, refrigerate the remains immediately. I use 1 pint jars.

7. Variation: Some people really like a sweet tomato sauce (my wife included). If this is your taste, then you can add 1 tablespoon of white sugar and 1 tablespoon of brown sugar when you first start simmering the sauce and adjust from there if you want it sweeter. As an alternative, you could also use a sweet red wine such a port or Marsala.

Get inspired with a Mediterranean Diet Breakfast

In case breakfast for you has been dry cereal or toast and butter, it is time for you to try out the cuisine of sunny countries that lie along the coast of Mediterranean Sea, such as Greece, Morocco, Italy, Spain and so on. You are bound to get inspired and opt for expanding your breakfast options. When we are talking of a Mediterranean breakfast, it would envisage big portion size of whole grains along with various seasonal fruits and even vegetables. There would be little quantities of milk and yogurt accompanying it. Do not be surprised by some few helpings of cheese or even eggs. This is not all. Sweetness and flavor will come your way through olive oil, various seeds and nuts, in addition to fresh honey, herbs besides spices and healthy fats.

There are certain guidelines which need to be followed in case of a Mediterranean Diet Breakfast. It has to comprise of fresh and unprocessed foods that are a rich source of complex carbohydrates as these will form the mainstay of this diet. Next, this is a plant based diet. Thus there will be fruits and vegetables, besides grains, nuts, as well as olive oil and even seeds that will be the basis of this daily diet. There will be fish, yogurt, in addition to milk, cheese, and eggs or poultry too but these will occupy only a much smaller portion of this meal according to the Mediterranean Diet Pyramid previously featured in this book. There is a limit with regard to red meat that will be served only a few times each month. Due to this variety of foods being included in this Mediterranean diet, it becomes possible to create simple breakfasts that are abundant in taste, nutrients, and textures.

The reason why the Mediterranean diet has become so popular is because ancient dietary patterns are being used. **They provide the benefit of increasing longevity in addition to improving of cardiovascular health**. After all, there is more focus on fresh and unprocessed foods. This means that you would be getting complex carbohydrates which are low in fat as well as unsaturated fats. Such kind of nutritional principles help to promote your overall well-being. In addition, even chronic diseases are prevented this way like previously stated. Basically this kind of food group proportions for breakfast corresponds to the guidelines for any balanced morning meal. This is a breakfast that comprises of a whole-grain cereal or even bread, a lean protein in some form, a dairy product, in addition to any seasonal fruit or a vegetable. There will be a plant-based fat to supply you with sustained energy, besides improving your concentration. You can control your weight as well as manage your cholesterol levels this way.

Certain basics of breakfast have been maintained in a Mediterranean diet. This means that you need to have whole grain breads along with cereals in addition to some fresh vegetable or fruit in your Mediterranean diet. Next you need to include yogurt, milk, in addition to eggs or even fish besides nuts and seeds and good fats to the breakfast. Choose from the various deeply pigmented fruits available. These would include apricots, oranges, besides figs, plums, and grapes. You may choose berries, apples or even pears. These are the fruits that can provide you with vitamins A, C, besides folate and potassium. And you also get the benefit of antioxidant compounds that are required to protect your body from heart disease and even cancer. With breads and cereals you are getting complex carbohydrates along with fiber. Thus you get energy along with healthy digestion. Also, by consuming low fat yogurt or even milk besides fish mean that you are getting protein and calcium too. There is the benefit of getting polyunsaturated as well as monounsaturated fats from olive oil, walnuts, besides the pistachios and almonds included in this diet. These help to improve the cardiovascular health in order to reduce the risks of cardiac disease.

There are various sample menus for you to choose from. A classic one would include ripe apricot halves covered with Greek yogurt. You can sprinkle honey and chopped pistachio nuts on it and serve this with whole-grain toast. Next, warm, whole oats can be had. Or else, try out brown rice along with milk. You may add cinnamon, almonds along with some raisins to it. This will be a hearty and nutritious morning breakfast for you. In case a portable breakfast is what you are looking for, then you can try out a sandwich which is made out of focaccia bread. Add some soft goat cheese to it. Put in some fresh tomato slices. Add on a few basil leaves. If you are keen for a high-protein breakfast, then add scrambled egg. Add some spinach along with scallions, finely chopped. And if you are looking for complex carbohydrates to provide energy, serve some eggs and whole grain bread. Have red grapes too.

Fruits:

Residents of Greece, for example, eat as much as nine servings of fruits each day and very little meat. This lowers the levels of low density lipoprotein or LDL, the bad cholesterol that is responsible for building deposits and choking the arteries.

Removing butter along with margarine from the breakfast table means reducing the calories, cholesterol, along with saturated animal fats besides trans fats in the morning breakfast. These trans fats are usually present in margarines besides the other butter substitutes. These tend to decrease good cholesterol but raise your "bad" cholesterol. So when you are transitioning to this diet, you need to remove butter or margarine. You may make use of light olive oil. Or else you may use some little amount of honey. Even some fruit preserves can be used.

Do ensure that they contain no added sugar. You can even have a kind of Mediterranean alternative to your toast and butter that is colorful too. Just have a whole grain roll toasted. Now spread some ricotta cheese on it, which is low in fat. Top this cheese with some fresh blackberries.

Or else you may add sliced strawberries to it. Add on some fig, currant or even apricot spread as that will also do wonders to your Mediterranean breakfast here. Enjoy a healthier lifestyle now!

Delicious Mediterranean Breakfast Pitas Recipe

This makes a yummy and delicious health breakfast or a snack for any time during the day. This is a low fat recipe that contains a mix of healthy ingredients like veggies and pepper to start your morning with a tasty Mediterranean pita.

Ingredients:

- 1/4 cup chopped sweet red pepper
- 1/4 cup of organic onion chopped
- 1 cup egg substitute
- 1/8 teaspoon salt
- 1/8 teaspoon pepper
- 1 small organic chopped tomato
- 1/2 cup torn fresh baby spinach

- 2 tbsp. of crumbled feta cheese
- 1-1/2 teaspoons minced fresh basil
- 2 whole pita breads

Method:

- Cook & stir onion and red pepper using a small cooking pan previously coated with cooking spray. Cook over medium heat for approx. three mints. In the meantime, in a medium size bowl, whisk the egg substitute, Mediterranean Sea salt and pepper. Add egg mix to skillet; cook and stir till it has consistency.
- Mix spinach, basil and tomato; arrange on pitas. Cover with egg substitute mix and sprinkle with feta cheese. Now it is ready to be served! Serves: 2

Nutritional Facts: approx. 265 calories for one pita, 2 g fat (1 g saturated fat), 4 mg cholesterol, 798 mg sodium, 41 g carbohydrate, 3 g fiber, 20 g protein. Diabetic Exchanges: 2 starch, 2 lean meats, 1 vegetable.

PREP TIME 25 MINS

YOUR NOTES

Yummy Mediterranean Breakfast Quinoa

Delicious cinnamon quinoa with toasted almonds, apricots, dates, and honey

Ingredients:

- 1/4 cup chopped raw almonds
- 1 teaspoon ground cinnamon
- 1 cup of quinoa
- 2 cups of low fat milk
- 1 teaspoon of Mediterranean Sea salt
- 2 tablespoons honey
- 1 teaspoon vanilla extract
- 2 dried pitted dates, finely chopped
- 5 dried apricots, finely chopped

Method:

1. Toast the almonds in a skillet over medium heat until just golden, approx. three to five mints; set apart.

2. Heat both the quinoa and the cinnamon together in a pan over medium heat until warmed through. Add the milk and the Mediterranean Sea salt to the pan and stir; bring the blend to a boil, ease the heat to low, cover the pan, and allow cooking at a simmer for approx. 15 minutes. Stir the dates, vanilla, apricots, honey, and about 1/2 the almonds into the quinoa mix. Cover with the remaining almonds to serve.

This yummy breakfast is ready in 25 minutes; you can also use raisins if you want for this recipe.

Delicious and Healthy Greek Yogurt Parfaits

This Greek Yogurt Parfaits makes a delicious and nutritious breakfast or snack. The polished whole berries from durum semolina wheat are known as "grain" in Italian and you can buy them in healthy specialized stores or at Italian markets. You can also use granola for this yummy breakfast recipe.

Ingredients:

- 12 cups water (divided)
- 1/4 cup orange blossom honey
- 1/4 tsp. of salt
- 4 cups of Greek style yogurt (plain 2%)

- Two cups of organic berries (fresh blueberries, blackberries or sliced strawberries)

Method:

1. Soak "grano" in 6 cups water overnight. Drain. Place in a medium saucepan with remaining 6 cups water over medium-high heat; bring to a boil. Ease the heat, and simmer 20 minutes or until "grano" is fairly tender. Drain well. Stir in honey and salt. Cool to room temperature. (or you can use granola instead)

2. Spoon approx. 1/4 cup yogurt into each of 8 glass cups. Top yogurt with three tbsp. of "grano" (or granola) and 2 tbsp. of berries. Put additional layers with the remaining ingredients.

Delicious Mediterranean Fritatta

This is a marvelous recipe to gather with friends and family on a relaxed weekend where you can enjoy plenty of time in a very Mediterranean lifestyle attitude so you can taste and share with your loved ones.

Ingredients:

- 8 kalamata olives (pitted, chopped)
- 1 zucchini (cut into 1/2 inch cubes)
- 1 red pepper (sweet, diced)
- 1/2 cup of chopped organic onions
- 1/4 cup of extra virgin olive oil
- 9 organic eggs (lightly beaten)
- 4 oz. crumbled feta cheese

- 1/3 cup of fresh thinly sliced basil
- 1/2 tsps. pepper
- 1/2 tsps. Of Mediterranean Sea salt
- 1/3 cup freshly grated parmesan (cheese)

Method:

1. Cook the first 4 ingredients in hot olive oil in a 10" oven-proof skillet over medium-high heat, stirring constantly until vegetables turn tender.
2. Mix eggs and next 4 ingredients, pour over vegetables in skillet.
3. Cover and cook over ½ -low heat 10-12 minutes or until almost set.
4. Take away from heat, and sprinkle with low fat Parmesan cheese.
5. Broil 5-1/2" from heat with oven door partially open approx. for 2 to 3 minutes or until golden brown
6. Cut frittata into even slices.

Preparation time: 45 minutes

Cooking time: 35 minutes

Serves: 6

Approx. calories per serving 280

Delicious and Healthy Mediterranean Tuna Fish Salad

This is a super healthy recipe for your weight loss purposes and it contains essential omega-3 fatty acids. In fact in many recent studies it has been demonstrated that eating a diet rich in omega-3 fatty acids combined with a regular exercise routine will give you the desired results even faster. This type of healthy fat helps to improve your blood flow naturally so that muscle functions improve and you shed more calories when exercising. This makes a great recipe for an easy to prepare lunch on the go loaded with delicious albacore, shredded fresh lettuce, sliced organic tomatoes and accompanied with Greek-style pita Chips.

Ingredients:

- 1 (12- oz.) can <u>albacore tuna</u> in water, drained and flaked into big chunks
- 1/2 cup of finely sliced organic red onion
- 2 organic celery stalks, finely sliced
- 2 tbsp coarsely chopped pitted <u>kalamata olives</u>
- 2 1/2 tbsp. of fresh organic lemon juice
- 1 tbsp. of extra virgin olive oil
- 2 big sliced organic tomatoes
- 1/4 teaspoon of freshly ground black pepper
- 1/8 teaspoon of Mediterranean Sea salt

Method:

1. Combine first 4 ingredients in a medium bowl. Add lemon juice and next 3 ingredients; toss gently to combine. Serve salad over sliced tomatoes.

Delicious Mediterranean Salad with Summer Beans and Feta

This is an amazing salad recipe from Italy where it is very popular and made using delicious and fresh tomatoes that evoke the Tuscany region and its beautiful hillsides. This recipe has yellow wax beans and feta cheese that give this refreshing and healthy salad a mild salty delicious flavor. Enjoy it as a super healthy low calorie dish to be incorporated in your weight loss diet plan.

Ingredients:

- 6 oz. coarse-textured rustic bread, 3 to 4 days old
- Mediterranean Sea salt and freshly ground black pepper
- 1/2 lb. of organic green beans, cut into 1-inch pieces
- 1/2 lb. of organic yellow wax beans, cut into 1-inch pieces
- 3 medium red organic tomatoes, seeded and cut into 3/4-inch dice

- 3 medium yellow organic tomatoes, seeded and cut into 3/4-inch dice
- 1 small red onion, cut into 1/2-inch dice
- 1/4 cup fresh organic basil leaves, lightly packed
- 1 Tbsp. coarsely chopped fresh oregano
- 5 Tbsp. red-wine vinegar
- 1/3 cup extra-virgin olive oil
- 12 oz. of crumbled feta cheese
- 2 cloves of minced organic garlic

Method:

Cut the bread into one inch pieces. Sprinkle with 1/2 cup water and let it rest for two minutes. Squeeze the bread with care till is dry. Tear it into one inch pieces and let it sit on paper towels for approx. 20 minutes.

Boil water into a big saucepan. Add the green and yellow beans and cook until it has a tender consistency but still crunchy, approx. three to five minutes. Drain and let it cool.

Arrange the onions, the tomatoes, the green and yellow beans (cooled) and the bread in a big serving dish. Shred the basil into 1/2-inch portions and toss carefully into the dish alongside with the oregano.

In a small dish, whisk together garlic, the vinegar and oil. Spice it up with Mediterranean Sea salt and pepper. Toss the salad with the vinaigrette and let it sit for approx. 20 minutes. Arrange the crumbled feta on top to serve and enjoy!

Delicious Couscous and Pomegranate Salad

Ingredients:

- 1 cup couscous
- boiling water
- 1 tbsp. of extra virgin olive oil
- 2 tsps. sherry wine vinegar
- 1/2 tsps. Mediterranean sea salt
- 1 tsp. lemon juice
- 1 cup of diced dried apricot
- 2 1/2 cups pomegranate seeds
- 1 diced organic green pepper
- 1 cup of organic cauliflower

Method:

1. Arrange the couscous in a big mixing dish. Add extra virgin olive oil, cauliflower, vinegar, Mediterranean Sea salt and lemon juice. Stir.

2. Pour boiling water over the couscous until just covered. Stir. Add more pure water if you notice that the couscous is still dry. Cover dish and let it rest for approx. six mins.

3. With a fork fluff the couscous. Depending on the couscous consistency, add more pure water, cover and let sit another few minutes.

4. Add pomegranate seeds and green pepper.

Serves 2

Prep Time: 10 minutes

Cook Time: 10 minutes, tot time: 20 mins.

Delicious Salmon Niçoise Salad with Kalamata Vinaigrette

This delicious riff on a Niçoise salad—minus the hard-cooked eggs and with salmon instead of tuna—comes together in about 30 minutes when you have leftover Cedar-Planked Salmon

Ingredients for vinaigrette:

- 6 Tbs. extra-virgin olive oil
- 1/3 cup Kalamata olives, pitted and minced (about 1/4 cup)
- 3 Tbs. white balsamic vinegar
- 1 medium clove garlic, finely grated
- 1/2 tsp. finely grated lemon zest

- 1/2 tsp. crushed red pepper flakes (optional)
- Mediterranean Sea salt and freshly ground black pepper

Salad Ingredients:

- 3/4 lb. baby red potatoes (each about 1-1/2 inches in diameter), cut into quarters
- Mediterranean Sea salt and freshly ground black pepper
- 1/2 lb. green beans, trimmed and cut into 1-1/2-inch lengths
- 1/2 lb. cherry or grape tomatoes (preferably mixed colors), halved
- 1/2 small red onion, thinly sliced
- 1/2 medium fennel bulb, cored and thinly sliced
- 2 cups baby arugula
- Freshly ground black pepper
- 3/4 lb. Cedar-Planked Salmon (or other cooked salmon fillets), skin removed, cut into 4 pieces, at room temperature

----

Vinaigrette preparation

In a small bowl, mix the oil, garlic, olives, vinegar, lemon zest, and red pepper flakes. Whisk to mix and season to taste with salt and pepper. Set apart.

Salad Preparation:

Arrange the potatoes in a cooking pan, cover with 2/4 of pure water, add 1 Tbsp. of Mediterranean Sea salt, boil over high heat. Ease the heat to medium and simmer gently until the potatoes acquire tender consistency when poked with a fork, approx. 5 minutes. Using a slotted spoon, move the potatoes to a big dish (save the cooking fluid).

 Whisk the vinaigrette to remix, drizzle 2 Tbsp. of it over the potatoes, sprinkle with Mediterranean Sea salt and pepper, and toss well. Set away and let cool to ambient temp.

 Boil the water in the cooking pan over high heat. In the meantime, fill a large dish with iced H2O. Put the green beans into the boiling water and cook until bright green and no longer raw but still very crisp, approx. 1 to 2 minutes. Drain the beans in a colander and plunge them into the iced H2O to halt the cooking. Drain one more time and arrange the beans on a clean dishtowel to dry them.

 Once potatoes are cooler, add the tomatoes, green beans, fennel, onion and all but 3 Tbsp. of the vinaigrette and toss well. Spice it up to taste with Mediterranean Sea salt and pepper. Add the arugula and toss gently. Transfer to a platter and top with the salmon. Drizzle with the remaining vinaigrette and now it is ready to serve and enjoy!

More Delicious and Healthy Recipes & Tips

Tip: Lower Your Cholesterol by Consuming Heart-Healthy Fats

It is essential for those who want to follow the **Mediterranean Diet** to consume the right type of fat. This means that in order to maintain and improve your nutrition with a heart-healthy diet you should incorporate monounsaturated fats in most of your recipes as the main source of fat. This will decrease the risk of having heart disease and also will give you all the benefits of this type of healthy fats like the extra-virgin olive oil where monounsaturated fats are predominantly found. Of course incorporating olives into your healthy diet is another option you have if you want to really supercharge your healthy fats consumption. Both olive oil and olives are a wonderful source of healthy anti-oxidants that help to reduce the risk of cancer and heart related disease. Eliminate trans fats completely from your menus, these type of fats increase your levels of bad cholesterol and increase the risk of heart disease.

Tip: How You Can Incorporate More Olive Oil into Your Healthy Diet:

The uses of olive oil are virtually unlimited when it comes to healthy cooking. This wonderful nature-based oil can be used in a number of different ways like the base for delicious vinaigrettes or you can drizzle the olive oil over lightly cooked vegetables. The fact is that this type of healthy oil has many applications when cooking, you can rub it on seafood, on vegetables and meats.

Another delicious and super healthy option is to dip your breads in a plate with olive oil and some drops of red wine, this will make your bread taste delicious! Always replace butter with extra-virgin olive oil for a much healthier diet.

Another great use of this wonderful ingredient for cooking is to drizzle olive oil over pasta and toss with freshly sliced basil leaves and freshly grated parmesan cheese. Replace butter when baking with olive oil.

You will be delighted when you start to use more olive oil more often into your healthy diet.

The following are examples of healthy recipes that incorporate olive oil and that are good for your heart-healthy and weight loss diet.

Delicious & Healthy Roasted Pumpkin and Feta Salad

Serves 4

Ingredients:

- 4 cups peeled, sliced sugar pumpkin (or winter squash)
- 1 tbsp. of extra-virgin olive oil
- Sea salt and freshly ground black pepper to taste
- 3 tbsp. of balsamic and olive oil vinaigrette
- 1 tbsp. of warmed organic honey
- 5 oz. (140 g) (0.31 pounds) of crumbled feta cheese
- 1 clove of garlic, chopped
- 1 bag mixed organic salad greens
- 2 tbsp. of toasted sliced almonds
- 1 teaspoon dried oregano

Method:

1. Preheat oven to 350 degrees F. (176 Celsius) Coat pumpkin with olive oil and season with pepper and sea salt. Arrange on a baking sheet and roast in the oven for approximately 20 minutes or until tender. Set apart and let it cool to room temperature.

2. Whisk together garlic, hone and vinaigrette in a large bowl. Toss with feta cheese. Add veggies and pumpkin and toss lightly to coat. Serve onto plates and garnish with almonds and oregano.

This delicious and colorful super healthy recipe is rich in antioxidants, full of flavor and an easy to prepare dish to be enjoyed at any time during the day. You can make this a wonderful heart-healthy meal by incorporating a good glass of red wine, enjoy!

Delicious Garlic Stuffed Olive and Tomato Bruschetta

Serves 8 to 10

Ingredients:

- 1 small loaf Ciabatta bread, sliced into 2-inch thick pieces
- 1/4 cup (2 oz.) of extra virgin-olive oil
- 1/2 jar garlic-stuffed olives, roughly chopped
- two cups (16 oz.) of chopped, seeded fresh vine ripe tomatoes
- Sea salt and freshly ground black pepper to taste
- A few leaves fresh basil, ripped
- 1 bunch of arugula, washed, patted dry

Method:

1. Preheat oven to 350 degrees F. (176 Celsius) Brush bread with olive oil and place on a baking sheet. Arrange in the oven and toast until light golden around the edges, 8 minutes approx.

2. In the meantime, mix together olives, sea salt, pepper and tomatoes to prepare the topping. Toss with arugula just before serving.

3. To serve, arrange the warm toasts on a plate and spread topping on toasts. Garnish with basil.

This easy and wonderful tasty recipe is a mouthwatering healthy dish that can be served as an appetizer. It has all the components of a heart-healthy recipe like olive oil, leafy greens, garlic and olives. Enjoy the textures of this delicious recipe by spreading it on a crispy toast. Enjoy!

**

Tip: Lower your consumption of saturated fats by replacing red meats with other type of proteins like beans, turkey, skinless chicken and fish. Eating fish at least two twice a week will incorporate a type of healthy fat (omega-3s) that is great for your heart health. Other great choices are tuna and salmon. Remember to use extra-virgin olive oil to cook your fish and serve with some veggies like broccoli.

Tip: Make veggies your favorite snack. The ideal consumption of vegetables in a day is 3 to 8 servings. You can reach this level of veggie consumption by incorporating more veggies from the start of the day. A great idea is to prepare a delicious spinach and veggie omelet in the mornings and have a veggie soup as a complement of your Mediterranean diet lunch. Any time you feel some cravings pick some healthy veggies like carrots, cucumbers or cauliflowers to eat as a healthy snack. Always eat one or two green salads during the day in between meals to maintain a high metabolic rate and to be sure your veggie intake is increased.

Tip: Eat more whole-grain pasta, grains and bread. Eating more whole-grains will increase your intake of dietary fiber hence improving your digestive system ability to eliminate more fat, lower your cholesterol levels and helping you to get rid of those unwanted extra pounds. More fiber consumption will also reduce your risk of heart disease. Look for "whole grain" and "whole wheat" in the packaging of the pasta you buy. Avoid refined products like refined pasta, this type of pasta lacks much of the fiber required for a much healthier diet. Avoid refined grains that contain too much complex carbohydrates that have a reduced nutritious value and make you fat. The problem is that the process of refining foods remove much of the fiber your system needs in order to reduce weight. Also when you consume foods that lack fiber your blood sugar levels can quickly increase. Another benefit of incorporating more fiber into your diet is that when consumed you feel full because it swells in your stomach after it absorbs liquid.

Tip: Make nuts and seeds part of your daily snacks: replace chips and cookies with almonds, sunflower seeds and walnuts. Refined snacks like cookies and chips are usually full of refined sugars and artificial sweeteners or trans fats. Of course other super healthy snacks are fresh fruits like grapes and strawberries if you crave for something sweet. You can enjoy a delicious bowl of strawberries with honey at any time during the day.

Tip: always incorporate fruit as a super healthy dessert. Indulge your palate with healthy and refreshing fresh fruits that are full of fiber and antioxidants. Always keep fruit within reach so whenever you have a sugar craving you can enjoy one of these healthy nature snacks like a pear or an apple instead of an unhealthy refined snack.

Tip: never forget to keep your body hydrated by drinking generous amounts of water during the day. Water cleanses your system and it also helps you feel full.

Tip: Incorporate exercise 3 times a week to boost your weight loss efforts significantly. Low impact exercising like walking or a bike ride or a simple walk through the park can boost your metabolic rate and also relax you and relax your mind. When you are stressed you tend to win more weight and tend to eat more, so relax and enjoy short walks as much as you can.

Tip: enjoy your meals, don't rush your food into your system, slow down a bit and enjoy the flavors of the Mediterranean diet. When you eat slowly you are tuning your brain signals of hunger with the fullness signal.

Tip: foods to avoid: refined flour and refined sugars, saturated fats (butter, margarines), desserts full of refined sugars like candies, fatty cuts of meat, fast foods and fried foods.

Tip: remember, the Mediterranean diet is no about counting calories, it is about a healthy and sustainable way of eating with good nutrients. Just remember to keep adequate portion sizes, not to big but not so small that you'll crave for more food 30 minutes after you eat.

Delicious Grilled Eggplant & Tomato Stacks

Serves: 6

Time: 25 minutes

Ingredients:

- 2 tsp. + 1 tablespoon extra-virgin olive oil, divided
- 1 medium eggplant (3/4-1 pound), cut into 6 rounds about 1/2 inch thick
- 1/2 teaspoon coarse salt, divided
- 6 tsp. prepared pesto
- 2 large organic tomatoes, each cut into 3 slices about 3/4 inch thick

- 4 ounces of fresh mozzarella, cut into 6 thin slices
- 6 fresh basil leaves
- 1 tbsp. of balsamic vinegar
- 1/4 teaspoon freshly ground pepper

Method:

Preheat grill to medium-high or place a grill pan over medium-high heat until hot.

Brush both sides of eggplant slices with 2 teaspoons of olive oil; sprinkle with 1/4 teaspoon of sea salt. Grill the eggplant slices for approx. five minutes. Turn; continue grilling until tender and marked with grill lines, 3 to 5 minutes more. Move to a large platter.

Spread each eggplant slice with 1 tsp. of pesto. Top with a slice of tomato, a slice of mozzarella and a basil leaf.

Drizzle vinegar and the remaining 1 tbsp. of oil over the towers; sprinkle with the remaining 1/4 teaspoon salt and pepper.

Note: You can grill the eggplant rounds up to 1 day in advance, then assemble the mozzarella, eggplant and tomato "stacks" at the end. Use tomatoes and eggplant with approx. the same diameter so the stack looks symmetrical.

Nutritional Information:

Per serving: 145 calories; 11 g fat (4 g sat); 17 mg cholesterol; 7 g carbohydrates; 0 g added sugars; 6 g protein; 3 g fiber; 323 mg sodium; 309 mg potassium.

Delicious Sweet Potato and Red Pepper Pasta

Serves: 4

Time: 30 minutes

Ingredients:

- 8 oz. (1 cup) of whole-wheat angel hair pasta
- 2 tbsp. extra-virgin olive oil, divided
- 4 cloves of organic garlic, minced
- 3 cups shredded, peeled sweet potato, (about 1 medium)
- 1 large red bell pepper, thinly sliced
- 1 cup diced plum tomatoes
- 1/2 cup water
- 2 tbsp. chopped fresh parsley
- 1 tbsp. chopped fresh tarragon
- 1/2 cup crumbled goat cheese
- 1 tbsp. white-wine vinegar, or lemon juice
- 3/4 teaspoon of sea salt

Method:

Boil water in a large pot. Cook pasta (use whole wheat grain pasta) until just tender (al-dente), 4 to 5 minutes approx. (see package instructions)

In the meantime, place 1 tbsp. of garlic and extra-virgin olive oil in a large skillet. Cook over medium heat, stirring occasionally, until the garlic is sizzling and fragrant, 2 to 5 minutes. Add tomatoes, sweet potato, bell pepper, and water and cook, stirring sporadically, until the bell pepper has a tender-crisp consistency, 5 to 7 minutes approx. Move away from heat, cover and keep warm.

Drain the pasta, reserving 1/2 cup of the cooking water. Return the pasta to the pot. Add parsley, the vegetable mixture, the remaining 1 tablespoon oil, oregano, vinegar (or lemon juice), sea salt and goat cheese; toss to combine. Add the reserved pasta water, two tbsp. at a time until the desired consistency is achieved.

Nutritional Information:

Per serving: 402 calories; 12 g fat (3 g sat); 7 mg cholesterol; 62 g carbohydrates; 0 g added sugars; 12 g protein; 9 g fiber; 546 mg sodium; 738 mg potassium.

This is a great way to incorporate your vegies with whole wheat pasta in a delicious and healthy dish full of herbs. Here's a way to use the "power vegetables" sweet potato and red bell pepper in a satisfying vegetarian pasta dish full of fresh herbs and creamy goat cheese. This delicious recipe can be accompanied by a healthy salad and a glass of red wine. Enjoy!

Super Easy & Fast Tuna Salad with Olives

Ingredients:

- 1 small sweet onion, or 1/2 a large, diced
- 4 stalks of organic celery, diced
- 3/4 cup pickle relish
- 1/4 cup salad olives, chopped
- 4 small cans tuna, drained well
- juice of 1 lemon
- 2 tbsp. of Dijon mustard
- 2 hardboiled eggs, chopped, optional
- 1/2 cup of plain Greek yogurt
- 1 tbsp. of extra-virgin olive oil
- Seal salt and pepper to season

Method:

Flake the tuna on a bowl then add all ingredients. Mix well. Refrigerate until ready to serve. You can serve on toast or combine with some greens. This is a great salad to make a healthy sandwich. Use wheat bread.

Delicious and Super Healthy Mediterranean Portobello Burger

flickr: (http://www.flickr.com/photos/shockinglytasty/6974559808/)

Serves: 4

Time: 30 minutes

Ingredients:

- 1 clove garlic, minced
- 1/2 tsp. of sea salt
- 2 tbsp. of extra-virgin olive oil, divided
- 4 portobello mushroom caps, stems and gills removed
- 4 large slices country-style whole wheat bread (sliced in half)
- 1/2 cup chopped organic tomato
- 1/2 cup sliced jarred roasted red peppers
- 1/4 cup crumbled reduced-fat feta cheese
- 2 tbsp. chopped pitted Kalamata olives
- 2 cups (16 oz.) of mixed baby salad greens
- 1 tbsp. of red-wine vinegar
- 1/2 tsp. dried oregano

Method:

1. Preheat grill to medium-high.
2. Make a smooth paste by mashing sea salt and garlic on a cutting board with the side of a knife. Mix the paste with 1 tbsp. of extra-virgin olive oil in a small dish. Lightly brush the oil mixture over portobellos and then on one side of each slice of the whole wheat bread.
3. Combine olives, feta, red peppers, tomato, vinegar, oregano and the remaining 1 tbsp. of olive oil in a medium bowl.
4. Grill the mushroom caps until tender, approx. four minutes per side; grill the bread until crisp, approx. one minute per side.
5. Toss salad greens with the red pepper mixture. Arrange the grilled mushrooms top-side down on 4 half-slices of the bread. Top with the salad mixture and the remaining bread. Enjoy!

Tip: You can add a slice of delicious and juicy pineapple to this yummy portabella burger to make it juicer and tastier!

Nutritional Information:

Per serving: 301 calories; 11 g fat (2 g sat); 2 mg cholesterol; 40 g carbohydrates; 10 g protein; 4 g fiber; 795 mg sodium; 691 mg potassium.

Delicious Grilled Mediterranean Salmon Skewers

Serves: 4 (Two skewers for each)

Time: 30 minutes

Ingredients:

- 2 tsp. of extra-virgin olive oil
- 2 tsp. of minced fresh rosemary
- 2 cloves of organic garlic, minced
- 1 tsp. of freshly grated lemon zest

- 1 tsp. lemon juice
- 1/2 tsp. of sea salt
- 1/4 tsp. of freshly ground pepper
- 1 pint cherry tomatoes
- 1 pound center-cut salmon fillet, skinned and cut into 1-inch cubes

Method:

1. Preheat grill to medium-high.
2. Mix lemon juice, sea salt, rosemary, extra-virgin oil, and garlic, pepper and lemon zest in a medium bowl. Add salmon; toss to coat. Alternating the salmon and tomatoes, divide among eight 12-inch skewers.
3. Oil the grill rack. Grill the skewers, carefully turning once, until the salmon is cooked through, approximately 4 to 6 minutes total. Serve immediately.

Note:

Arrange skewers (Step 2), cover and refrigerate for up to 8 hours. Continue with grilling (Steps 1 & 3) when ready to serve. | Equipment: Eight 12-inch skewers

How to remove skin from salmon fillet: Arrange skin-side down. Starting at the tail end, slip a long sharp knife between the skin and the fish flesh, holding down strongly with your other hand. Softly push the blade along at a 30° angle, separating the skin from the fillet from without cutting through either.

Oil the grill rack using an oiled folded paper towel by rubbing it over the rack.

Nutritional Information:

Per serving: 172 calories; 7 g fat (1 g sat); 53 mg cholesterol; 4 g carbohydrates; 0 g added sugars; 23 g protein; 1 g fiber; 200 mg sodium; 607 mg potassium

Delicious and Healthy Roasted Cod with Warm Tomato-Olive-Caper Tapenade

Serves: 4

Time: 20 minutes

Ingredients:

- 1 pound cod fillet
- 3 tsp. extra-virgin olive oil, divided
- 1/4 tsp. freshly ground pepper
- 1 tsp. minced shallot
- 1 cup halved cherry tomatoes
- 1/4 cup chopped cured olives
- 1 tsp. capers, rinsed and chopped
- 1 1/2 teaspoons chopped fresh oregano
- 1 tsp. balsamic vinegar

Method:

1. Preheat oven to 450°F. (230 Celsius) Coat a baking sheet with cooking spray.
2. Rub cod with 2 tsp. of extra-virgin olive oil. Sprinkle with pepper. Arrange on the prepared baking sheet. Move to the oven and roast until the fish flakes

easily with a fork, approx. 15 to 20 minutes, depending on the thickness of the fillet.

3. In the meantime, heat the remaining 1 tsp. of olive oil in a small skillet over medium heat. Add shallot and cook, stirring, until beginning to soften, approx. 20 seconds. Add cherry tomatoes and cook, stirring, until softened, about 1 1/2 minutes. Add olives and capers; cook, stirring, for 30 seconds more. Stir in oregano and vinegar; take away from heat. Spoon the tapenade over the cod to serve. Enjoy!

Nutritional Information:

Per serving: 151 calories; 8 g fat (1 g sat); 45 mg cholesterol; 4 g carbohydrates; 0 g added sugars; 15 g protein; 1 g fiber; 602 mg sodium; 335 mg potassium.

Delicious Greek Pasta Salad

Serves: 4

Time: 30 minutes

Ingredients:

- 1 cup penne pasta (use whole wheat pasta)
- 2 tbsp. red wine vinegar
- 1-1/2 tsp. lemon juice
- 1 clove garlic, crushed
- 1 tsp. dried oregano
- Sea salt and pepper to taste
- 1/3 cup extra-virgin olive oil
- 5 cherry tomatoes, halved
- 1/2 small red onion, chopped
- 1/2 green bell pepper, chopped
- 1/2 red bell pepper, chopped
- 1/4 cup crumbled feta cheese
- 1/4 cucumber, sliced
- 1/4 cup sliced black olives

Method:

1. Fill a large cooking container with lightly sea salted water (use Mediterranean Sea Salt) and bring to a rolling boil over high heat. Once the water is boiling, stir in the penne pasta, and return to a boil. Cook the pasta uncovered, sporadically stirring, until the pasta

has cooked through, but is still firm to the bite (al dente), approx. 11 minutes. Rinse with cold water and drain well in a colander set in the sink.

2. Whisk together garlic, oregano, the vinegar, lemon juice, sea salt, pepper, and olive oil. Set apart. Combine tomatoes, onion, pasta, green and red peppers, olives, feta cheese and cucumber in a large bowl. Pour vinaigrette over the pasta and combine together. Cover and chill for 3 hours approx. before serving. Enjoy!

Nutritional Information:

Calories 307 kcal 15% - Carbohydrates 19.3 g – Cholesterol 14 mg – Fat 23.6 g

Fiber 2.1 g – Protein 5.4 g

Delicious Mediterranean Pasta Salad

Prep Time: 15 minutes

Cook Time: 15 minutes

Serves: 4 servings

Ingredients:

- 8 oz of whole wheat organic farfalle
- Zest and juice of 1 lemon
- 1 organic grated carrot
- 2 tsp. of extra-virgin olive oil

- One 14 oz. can of artichoke hearts packed in water, drained and chopped
- 8 oz. fresh part-skim mozzarella cheese, chopped
- 1/4 cup chopped bottled roasted red bell pepper
- 1/4 cup chopped fresh parsley
- 1/2 cup frozen peas

Method:

1. Follow package instructions to cook pasta (al-dente).

2. While pasta cooks, mix zest and juice of 1 lemon and 2 teaspoons of extra-virgin olive oil in a large bowl; stir well with a whisk. Add artichoke hearts, grated carrot, bell pepper, and parsley and mozzarella cheese; toss to combine.

3. Arrange peas in a colander; when pasta is cooked, drain pasta over peas. Shake well to drain, but avoid running under cold water. Add peas and pasta to artichoke mix, and toss well until thoroughly combined. Serve warm or at room temperature.

Nutritional Information

Calories per serving: 420 - Fat per serving: 20g - Protein per serving: 20g - Carbohydrates per serving: 50g - Fiber per serving: 8g

How Much Weight Can You Lose With a Mediterranean Diet?

Many people tend to ask about weight loss concerning specific diets. After all, it's important to understand that weight loss can happen with certain diets, and if people work hard and are diligent about what they want and what they need, but it's not so simple when it comes to losing weight and getting the most out of your diet in a sustainable, healthy, and long-term fashion.

Specifically with the Mediterranean Diet, you can certainly lose weight, drop fat, drop pounds, and both look and feel better, but it's not that simple — after all, it's not about how much weight you can lose, or losing a set amount of weight, but more about **creating healthy and long-term sustainable habits with the diet itself** that can last you for years to come and ensure that you get the most out of the diet itself while improving your health and more over time.

The Mediterranean Diet is, in essence, a diet based on natural foods, olive oils, and seafood like fish that have healthy, fatty acids that can aid in weight loss and generally help you across the board. As such, the Mediterranean Diet tends to be one of the diets that are more legitimate and sustainable than others, and it is typically a diet that is ideal for people who are searching for something more than just the latest fad or trend that will fall out of favor in the coming weeks or months.

The Mediterranean Diet is ideal for people in a number of ways, but primarily it is perfect for those who are seeking a way to lose weight in a sustainable fashion, without resorting to bizarre fads or trends of any sort. After all, fads and trends generally don't stand the test of time in the weight loss industry, but solid diets like the

Mediterranean Diet do wonders when it comes to sustainable and long term weight loss.

People on this diet report to losing a good deal of weight over time, but more importantly, they report to keeping it off for good, and being able to move freely and effectively without worrying about their weight over time in the sense that they get the most out of their weight loss while enjoying their new found body in due time, as well.

For many people, it's no wonder that the Mediterranean Diet has become ideal – weight loss is a central component of it, but it really comes down to the fact that you don´t need to be an expert in weight loss, or somebody who works incredibly diligently – you just need to be someone who can take the time out of their day to commit to small steps in weight loss that reap big benefits over time. This type of food and cooking focuses more on nutritious values than adding unnecessary calories to your diet. Just by getting rid of a processed food based diet and by introducing this healthy way of cooking into your menus your body will start to reflect those changes in your eating habits with a slimmer and healthier figure.

Use the Mediterranean Diet for weight loss, and I am positive it will do miracles both for your health and ideal weight. There's a reason so many people have found long term success with it – it is both sustainable and worthwhile, and it works wonders when it comes to getting the most out of your new healthy, sustainable lifestyle.

Discover the Health and Fitness Benefits of Red Wine

Wine is one of the oldest alcoholic beverages on the planet today. The history of wine continues through the millennia and although excessive drinking of any type of alcohol causes numerous health problems and does not produce any benefits, today's research suggests that having a glass of red wine daily can provide you with something more than just simple relaxation.

Studies on the benefits of red wine have been going on for almost two centuries. Media has only begun to spread the news in the early nineties. The concept of 'French paradox' and the assumption that their alcohol consumption put away the French from cardiovascular disease despite the high consumption of animal fats reveals that the health benefits of red wine were known to man since early ages.

Among the more than 400 substances that make up red wine, the one that deserves a place of honor is **Resveratrol**. This is a **polyphenol antioxidant** found mostly in red wines and has a molecular structure very similar to the hormone estrogen. However, studies on the action of 'Resveratrol', one of the active ingredients in non-alcoholic red wine did not appear until 1997, when the researchers began to work on the ability of this substance to prevent cancer.

Resveratrol, according to many studies has the ability to improve the cell efficiency, enhancing the activity of mitochondria, i.e. the "energy units" found in cells. Some research conducted on animals also demonstrates that Resveratrol favors longevity, provides better control over diabetes, has a protective effect on the heart and blood circulation and also reactivates the metabolism.

Researchers have found that Resveratrol produces neuroprotective effects thus reducing the risk of Alzheimer's disease.

Here are some more benefits of red wine consumption if consumed in moderate quantities:

1. Reduction in the risk of death by almost all causes: European researchers suggest that a daily judicious

consumption of red wine (22-32 g of alcohol) has a suppressing effect on most of the causes of mortality. According to studies by UK, France, Denmark and Finland, drinking wine is much more beneficial than consuming beer or other spirits.

2. Tobacco:

Smoking seriously harms the very natural ability to relax the blood vessels or vasodilation. Red wine reduces the ill effects of tobacco on the endothelium, a tissue of cells that regulates a reduction in friction linings of the lymphatic vessels, blood vessels and heart.

3. Diseases of the heart:

One of the best known and most studied benefits of red wine is the protection of the heart. A moderate and regular consumption of red wine can act as prevention against coronary heart disease. The scientists claim that red wine limits the hazard of coronary heart ailment by boosting HDL or high-density lipoprotein levels and reducing the production of LDL or low-density lipoprotein.

4. Blood clotting:

Red wine carries out an anticoagulant or anti thrombosis action. The consumers of wine have a lower level of fibrin, the protein that promotes blood clotting.

5. Atherosclerosis:
Red wine can prevent the origin and development of atherosclerosis (hardening of the arteries). Atherosclerosis occurs when blood vessels begin to lose their ability to relax. The alcohol found in red wine helps in maintaining healthy blood vessels by facilitating the production of nitric oxide (NO), a chemical that is a fundamental relaxation factor.

6. Hypertension:
Excessive consumption of alcohol is generally considered risky for hypertension. However, there is some evidence on the beneficial effects of red wine on blood pressure. 250 ml or two glasses of red wine combined with meals have been found to lower blood pressure in persons suffering from hypertension.

7. Kidney stones:
The intake of red wine lowers the risk of stone formation in kidneys.

8. Red wine can reduce hunger:
Red wine also contains other elements important from the point of view of nutrition such as sugars and mineral salts (in the amount of about 2 grams per liter), in

addition to yeast, ferments and enzymes. In small doses, alcohol can have a soothing and reducing effect on hunger. A glass of wine also helps you to digest better because its pleasant taste and alcohol stimulate gastric and intestinal secretions.

So instead of drawing general conclusions and telling everyone that they should be drinking wine every day, it would be worthwhile to try it yourself if your current situation fits any one of the "at-risk" situations listed in the previous paragraphs. Red wine health benefits have been proven beyond certainty and a number of people across the globe are benefitting from them, so enjoy a good glass of wine with every one of your Mediterranean diet recipes now!

The Health Powers of Olive Oil

In the Mediterranean Diet and culture olive oil has a predominant presence over margarine or butter. The use of olive oil is widely spread as a healthy complement in salads, breads, vegetables, desserts and to cook fish. Unlike animal products like margarines and butters that are made from animal base materials, olive oil has monounsaturated fats that are excellent for your health;

this reduces the risk of having heart disease problems. The consumption of olive oil is excellent to maintain good cholesterol levels in order while controlling and lowering LDL levels (bad cholesterol). This healthy oil also provides **powerful antioxidants** in the form of **phytochemicals** to your system when consumed in the right quantities through a healthy Mediterranean diet.

This phytochemicals also help to lower your blood pressure levels. The regular consumption of olive oil helps to reduce bad cholesterol, LDL, and keep the good cholesterol, HDL, at optimal levels.

The Health Benefits of Olive Oil

1. Cardiovascular benefits of olive oil

Olive is a monounsaturated fat in nature (approx. 75% monounsaturated), this equips it with great benefits to the hearth .This is because it reduces the chances of blocking the vessels carrying the blood. It helps in maintaining open vessels for blood to flow in an unobstructed manner. This is highly important because all parts of the body will be in a good position to be supplied with necessary nutrients for its health requirements. Phytochemical is a useful chemical that is found in olive oil that benefits the body and enhances your system functions notably. Just by consuming enough of this oil on a regular basis you greatly increase the chances of fighting heart related diseases through the increase intake of the phytochemical ingredient in olive oil.

2. Regulating inflammation in the body

Oleocanthal is a useful component found in olive oil that helps your system to regulate inflammation .Inflammation can be a sign of defense against infection and injury but too much of it is dangerous. This is because it can cause diabetes or it can damage different organs in your body. To prevent the negative effects of too much inflammation in the body oleocanthal in olive oil plays a great role in regulating inflammation in your system to a desired level. There are several health complications that involve a lot of inflammation that ends up becoming a great health risk. Consuming high amounts of olive oil can help reduce the negative effect caused by excessive inflammation.

3. Treating cancer

There are many types of cancer that are associated with too much fat in the body or the type of fat consumed. Olive oil through research has proved to be beneficial in reducing the risks of cancer in the body. This type of vegetable oil has proved successful to treat different types of cancers such as colon cancer, breast cancer and prostate cancer. These cancers cause a lot of suffering to the people affected with these types of illnesses. Consuming this oil is highly beneficial as it leads to a much healthier condition free from many types of disorders and complications. Patients with this kind of cancers are highly encouraged to increase olive oil consumption for them to benefit more from its positive powers in fighting this disease.

4. Treating diabetes using olive oil

Diabetes is a complication that is associated with causing

severe variation in blood sugar level that can be fatal. Individuals suffering from this complication are supposed to be highly careful by engaging in activities and eating habits that will not increase their risks of increasing the sugar level in the blood. Possible suggestions that are there for people who are trying to regulate their blood sugar level naturally is through the adoption of healthy diets that will lead to low carbohydrates in their bodies. Through research it has been proved for diets rich in monounsaturated fats such as the Mediterranean Diet rich in olive oil to be more effective in helping these individuals regulate their blood sugar level in a natural and effective way.

5. Benefit of olive oil in weight loss

Excess body weight is directly related to too much cholesterol level in the body. It is highly discouraged due to the various and terrible effects it causes to an individual`s health. It increases chances of complications such as growing levels of heart disease and other ailments associated with obesity. The use of olive oil that is a monounsaturated fat in nature can help a lot in achieving an effective weight loss and controlling triglycerides. This is because the monounsaturated fats will work in reducing the levels of bad cholesterol and at the end reducing the negative effects of excess body weight which is highly beneficial to the body. It is an excellent alternative for cooking to replace margarines and butters as it is a vegetable based oil.

To get the most antioxidant powerful effects from this healthy vegetable oil you should opt for the **"extra-virgin" olive oil** which is less processed and even more beneficial for your health. A very powerful type of **omega-3 fatty acid** can also be obtained from the frequent consumption of another staple of the Mediterranean food such as canola oil and the regular intake of healthy nuts. A substance called linolenic acid contained in canola oil and some nuts are effective polyunsaturated and monounsaturated fats that help to lower your triglycerides in a natural way while preventing blood clotting improving the health of your blood vessels and regulating blood pressure. Some fishes that are commonly consumed in the Mediterranean region such as albacore tuna, salmon, mackerel and herring are excellent sources of omega-3 fatty acids.

THANK YOU FOR READING THIS BOOK AND I WISH YOU A HEALTHY LIFESTYLE! – ENJOY LIFE AND TAKE CARE OF YOUR HEALTH NOW!

As my gift to you, get a **FREE COPY** of the

Best Mediterranean Breakfast Recipes

And a healthy Diet Plan here:

http://mediterraneandietrecipes.blogspot.com/

MEDITERRANEAN DIET COOKBOOK

BEST RECIPES FOR HEALTHY WEIGHT LOSS

Best Seller
amazon.com

YOUR HEALTHY EATING COOKBOOK

WITH MORE RECIPES AND TIPS FOR BEGINNERS

DELICIOUS AND EASY HEALTHY RECIPES

MARIO FORTUNATO

Other Book Titles You May Like:

http://tinyurl.com/green-juicing-diet

http://tinyurl.com/clean-salad-recipes

The information contained in this book is for informational purposes only, and is in no way intended as medical advice or as a substitute for medical counseling. All content and information is provided as-is, and the reader assumes all risks from the use, non-use or misuse of this information. Neither the author or the publisher, partners or affiliates will be held accountable in any way for the use or misuse of the information provided herein. The author and publisher of this work are not medical doctors. This book is not to be considered, in any way medical advice. Because there is some risk involved to make any health changes, all the above mentioned persons involved with the development and distribution of this book are not responsible for any adverse effects or consequences of any kind resulting from the use or misuse of any suggestions or procedures described within this book. Always work with a qualified health professional before making any changes to your diet, prescription drug use, lifestyle or fitness activities.
None of the content should be relied on as a cure, preventive, or treatment for any disease or medical condition. It is recommended that you consult with a licensed medical doctor or physician before acting on any recommendations made in this book.

Health Disclaimer

Any and all information contained herein is not intended to take the place of medical advice from a health care professional. Any action taken based on these contents is at the sole discretion and sole liability of the reader.
Readers should always consult appropriate health professionals on any matter relating to their health and wellbeing before taking any action of any kind concerning health related issues. Any information or opinions provided here are believed to be accurate and sound, however the author assumes no liability for the use or misuse of information provided here.
The author will in any way be held responsible by any reader who fails to consult the appropriate health authorities with respect to their individual health care before acting on or using any information contained herein, and neither the author or publisher of any of this information will be held responsible for errors or omissions, or use or misuse of the information.

425R00108

Made in the USA
San Bernardino, CA
16 October 2014